Date Due

MAY 11 1972			
NOV 8 1972			
DEC 14 1973			
AUG 14 1974			
DEC 9 1974			
DEC 16 1974			

The Folk-Carol of England

THE FOLK-CAROL OF ENGLAND

DOUGLAS BRICE

HERBERT JENKINS
LONDON

First published 1967 by Herbert Jenkins Ltd
2 Clement's Inn, London WC2

Printed in Great Britain by
Robert Cunningham and Sons Ltd
Alva

TO

ELIZABETH POSTON

IN TRIBUTE AND ADMIRATION

OF HER SCHOLARSHIP AND

WORK AS A COMPOSER,

THIS VOLUME IS

RESPECTFULLY

DEDICATED

Contents

Preface

On the subject of folk-song there would seem to be less agreement among scholars than in any other department of musical history. A half a century has elapsed since the death of Cecil Sharp, yet there is still, in this field of study, little unanimity even among the most eminent of academicians. It is a thorny subject, and any uncompromising or dogmatic approach inevitably sparks off a discussion that generates more heat than light. It was a pity that so industrious and dedicated a pioneer as Cecil Sharp should also have been a man of so unrelenting a disposition, for he left behind him at his death a trail of bitterness that cost him the friendship of many who at one time had been among his most ardent admirers. It cannot be over-emphasized therefore that the first requisite in anyone devoting himself to work in the often impenetrable thicket of folk-song, is to keep the windows of his mind wide open. In a correspondence with Dom Gregory Murray (*Tablet*, 7th February 1959) Margaret Dean-Smith gives a practical example of the traps into which the over-confident can fall when she describes the scene at a typical gathering of folk-song enthusiasts:

Dom Gregory Murray refers to "oral tradition". One wonders whether he has ever attended a typical lecture given by a collector of the "old" Herderian school and heard the inevitable discussion arising on the usual proposal that "oral tradition" is a definitive characteristic of folk-song. "But", will object the first speaker to catch the chairman's eye, "'Tipperary' (*ac similiter*) exists in oral tradition; very few people know it by any other means, yet you say

'Tipperary' is not a folk-song: why?" And he probably adds for good measure that many of the hymns we love are known in the same way. The answer is seldom satisfactory to the questioner, and the chairman hastens to encourage someone else, who asks (inevitably), "What about obscene songs, which exist only in oral tradition, since they are unprintable?" The lecturer, true to Herder's dictum that folk-song does not exist in streets or alleys, whose inhabitants "only yell and destroy" denies that those are folk-songs: but others wise in "original versions" rise to recite folk-songs within the canon that are very ribald indeed. The chairman hopefully turns to a more sedate person, who refers to the classical music of India – the antithesis of folk-song, which is preserved only in oral tradition, and brings up a battery of other instances. Since it is evident that "oral tradition" cannot be a means of defining folk-song the chairman, out of regard for the lecturer, brings the discussion to a close. No one goes home satisfied.

The following pages are concerned principally with those folk-songs which relate exclusively to the Christmas story, the early encounters of the Holy Family, and the Life of Christ. It would be foolish in the extreme to claim that this volume is the last word on the subject; the door is still very wide open, and will continue to remain so, we think, for a very long time to come. The author however, has endeavoured to bring to this discussion something of that breadth of vision which he feels should always accompany any approach to a subject surrounded with so much uncertainty. Since the revival of the mediaeval carol these simple compendiums of Christian doctrine have had a very wide appeal and their popularity grows with every Christmas that passes. It is hoped that these chapters will stimulate the interest of an already sympathetic public, and be a help to the more knowledgeable who would like to know more.

Acknowledgements

In the composing of this volume the author wishes to express his heart-felt thanks to The English Folk-Song and Dance Society and to Ruth Noyes the Librarian at Cecil Sharp House for permission to make use of material – both words and music – made available to posterity through the industry of Anne Geddes Gilchrist, O.B.E., F.S.A., and Lucy Broadwood; and for the same reason to Dr Maud Karpeles, O.B.E., for permission to make use of Cecil Sharp's *English Folk-Song* (Heinemann, 1965, Ed. Dr Karpeles), his "Cherry Tree Ballad" with its tune from the Appalachians, and the "Wassail Song" from his *Folk-Songs from Somerset* (5th Series). Equally, the author is indebted to Mrs Vaughan Williams for permission to reproduce a pentatonic melody (*English Folk-Song*, p. 106), and to Margaret Dean-Smith, F.S.A., for her encouragement, invaluable help and information.

The author also wishes to thank the historian at Buckfast Abbey for permitting the use of his thesis on the "Adeste Fideles"; the Oxford University Press for permission to use two texts from the *Oxford Book of Carols*: Nos. 81 and 43 collated by Percy Dearmer; the editor of *The Month* for allowing the reprinting of poems by Barbara Rochford; the editor of the *Sunday Times* who so graciously consented to my use of the winning entry in the Competition of 1958; to Burns Oates and Washbourne for allowing the use of their *Anthology* compiled by Shane Leslie; to Miss D. E. Collins for the use of three poems by G. K. Chesterton; to J. M. Dent and Sons Ltd for permission to reprint "The Christ Child" from *The Wild Knight and other Poems*, and to Methuen and Co. Ltd for agreeing to the publication of "God Rest You Merry, Gentlemen" and two verses from "Songs of Education" (History), from *Collected Poems* (G. K. C.).

To the above-mentioned the following acknowledgements have also to be added: the author expresses his gratitude to the Rev. George Palmer, Rural Dean of Deddington, Oxford, not only for his assistance, but for the exceedingly courteous manner with which he met the varying needs of the author; to Michael Lee of Bramley, Leeds, and to the Rev. Leslie H. Bunn, B.A., and Honourable Editor for the Revision of *Julian's Dictionary of Hymnology*, for their advice on the subject of the *Arundel Hymnal*; to A. D. Peters and Co. for the reprinting of the "Noël" by Hilaire Belloc; to Sydney Carter for the inclusion of his lovely carol; to Sidgwick and Jackson Ltd, for the use of two fifteenth-century MS carols; to J. Curwen and Sons for consenting to the reproduction of the "In Dessexshire Ballad", and "The Twelve Joys" in an unusual version.

I feel that I should add that should I have offended – through an oversight – against copyright to the smallest degree, I apologize at once, and promise to have such matters rectified instantly, in all future editions of this volume.

Hitherto, acknowledgements have been confined to the demands of juridical copyright; there are others, no less important, that are due by virtue of ordinary Christian fidelity. The writer wishes to acknowledge the generous assistance contributed by Denis Crosby conductor of the Birmingham Choral Union; Mary Barber, MUS.B., L.R.A.M., A.R.C.M., of the B.B.C.; and of Elizabeth Barber pianoforte-mistress, who throughout half a century possesses the astounding record of having entered pupils for the Associated Board Examinations without sustaining a single failure.

There remains one final acknowledgement to include: I feel it is the most important of all. In Church Street at Lower Edmonton, North London, there stands the beautiful ivy-mantelled parish church of "All Saints" dating back to the fourteenth century – possibly earlier – where Mr Evill discharged with edifying devotion the duties of Vicar. In the vicinity of the churchyard where the mortal remains of Charles Lamb lie sheltered within the shade of the yew trees, stood a small Church-School of barely six classrooms. Here, at Latimer School, Mr Beardwall – a mountain of a man with a kindly nature – held the post of music-teacher. It was here, at this Church of England School, that I, now a Roman Catholic clergyman, spent the happiest years of my life. At the age of five years, under the quiet vigilance of Mr Beardwall, and with my hand in his, I took my first small steps into the beautiful world of music. At the age of fifty years, I cannot remember having loved anyone more. May he rest in peace; and may God have mercy on his kind and gentle soul.

DOUGLAS BRICE

Sweet Auburn! loveliest village of the plain;
Where health and plenty cheered the labouring swain,
Where smiling spring its earliest visit paid,
And parting summer's lingering blooms delayed:
How often have I paused on every charm,
The sheltered cot, the cultivated farm,
The never-failing brook, the busy mill,
The decent church that topped the neighbouring hill!
How often have I blessed the coming day,
When toil remitting lent its turn to play,
And all the village train, from labour free,
Led up their sports beneath the spreading tree.
The dancing pair that simply sought renown,
By holding out to tire each other down;
These were thy charms sweet village! sports like these,
With sweet succession, taught even toil to please:
These round thy bowers their cheerful influence shed;
These were thy charms – but all these charms are fled.
Ill fares the land, to hastening ills a prey,
Where wealth accumulates, and men decay:
Princes and lords may flourish, or may fade;
A breath can make them, as a breath has made;
But a bold peasantry, their country's pride,
When once destroyed, can never be supplied.

from "The Deserted Village"
by Oliver Goldsmith (1728-1774)

AUTHOR'S NOTE

The purely numerical references to standard works appearing in the Annotated Bibliography will, in the main, be of interest only to the academician; but the explanatory passages – for each of which an index-number may be found in the body of the text – form an essential part of the treatise, and assist the reader towards a more perfect understanding of the matter under survey. – D. B.

Introduction

As a forethought, and at the risk of appearing self-centred, it occurred to me that perhaps the reader of the following pages might be interested to learn of the rather unique incident as a result of which the following chapters came to be written. They were the outcome of a charming experience, the memory of which I feel sure will remain with me for the rest of my days, be they many or few.

A Londoner by birth, it has long been my delight as the Christmas season draws near, to leave my northern domicile and returning to the scene of my childhood to hear once again the carols sung in the streets of the London suburbs, around the giant Christmas tree in Trafalgar Square, and in the famous metropolitan churches, cathedrals, and concert halls. It was the Monday following the Third Sunday of Advent: I had boarded the train at Lime Street Station and had scarcely settled comfortably in a corner of an empty compartment when I was joined by a young lady of exotic beauty who, it was later disclosed was from the Argentine. Simply dressed, she presented an over-all picture of the type of Morisco gypsy to be met with in Andalusia and the districts of southern Spain. She smiled, asked if I was a Roman Catholic clergyman, and we soon became actively engaged in conversation. When in the course of the journey it became known that I was interested in music and particularly in the history of the carol, her large gazelle-like eyes opened, and her Moorish features lit up like an Andalusian dawn: "Ah, the carol! I love carols – please sing me some carols – *do* please sing me some carols!" she exclaimed in her stilted accent. This was something I had not anticipated, and an ordeal for which I was not prepared. However, after a great deal of persuasion I was compelled to give way, and with the welcome assurance that she would divert her gaze away from me to the ice-bound countryside without, and the prospect of an untimely visit from the ticket collector due to appear at any moment, in my choirboyish voice – somewhere between a light tenor and a treble, the recital commenced; and I sang, tentatively at first – "While Shepherds Watched". This I followed with "God Rest You Merry, Gentlemen", and gaining confidence continued with "The Cherry Tree Ballad", "A Virgin Most Pure", and "On Christmas Night all Christians Sing". I had scarcely concluded the last item when the audience forgot its promise, and turning to me exclaimed gleefully: "Ah, that was the Sussex song; that was lovely!" "Very nice it was Sir! – if I might say so; sing us another one!" exclaimed a martial voice that took me by surprise. To my great confusion it was the Inspector whose sudden arrival in my preoccupation I had not observed. I was in no state to oblige and was more than relieved at his ultimate departure.

It was this episode that on my way home from Euston Station (where incidentally, carol-singing was already in progress) induced me to think seriously about composing something on the subject of the Christmas Carol: that mysterious song-form, which sinking differences of colour, race, and creed, reduced all men to the same common denominator – not as understood in the false philosophy of Communism which repudiates the rights of the individual personality, but as children of God, and members of the same great Human Family.

At the beginning of the tenth chapter of the Third Book of Kings it is related that the Queen of Sheba undertook a long and tedious journey to hear the wisdom of King Solomon. Here in our own day was a simple Argentinian peasant girl who had come from the other side of the globe to spend the feast of Christmas in the very heart of the carol country, to hear once again the message of the angels, and to taste of wisdom at its very fount. Ships passing in the night – maybe; but the Holy Family were in those ships, the stars shone bright and the moon was up, as on the night of the first Christmas carol.

Chapter 1

The English Carol

One of the most wonderful experiences that can come the way of anyone living in the north-west of England is to be present in the Anglican cathedral in Liverpool for the annual Carol Service at Christmas time. Here, under Ronald Woan, the Master of Choristers, the visitor would be treated to a polished performance of some of the finest of our English carols. On an afternoon immediately preceding the feast of the Nativity that vast and beautiful building would be filled from end to end with ordinary working men and women, young boys and girls, mothers with infants on their knees – all listening attentively and in a well-behaved manner to a programme of Christmas carols that would go on for anything from three to four hours. An edifying and heartening sight!

It would be only natural, therefore, for an intelligent member of the congregation captivated by the simplicity and charm of the carol, to enquire after such a feast: what exactly is a carol, and how is it that it has such an appeal when compared with other forms of song such as the parochial hymn? Here we have two very intriguing questions proposed as one; but before attempting to answer them we should trace the carol to its earliest beginnings and study the etymology of the word itself.

The Rev. H. R. Bramley writing towards the close of the nineteenth century thought that the word "carol" came from the Greek "choros" meaning a round-dance[1]; but these were early and tendentious days, and in the years that followed, continual speculation produced a variety of opinions. Professor Rossell Hope Robbins believes that "carol" derives from the Latin word "chori" meaning "psalms for use in procession", and rather than trace its origin to the Italian "ballata" he sees its beginnings in the liturgy of the Sarum Rite and the worship of the English Church of the fifteenth century.[2] Rimbault thought that it was derived from the two Latin words – "cantare" meaning "to sing" and "rola" a common interjection.[3] Ecclesiastics on the other hand have sought its beginnings in the French word "kyrielle" meaning a circular dance which they trace to the "Kyrie eleison" of the Mass with its threefold invocation connoting the Christian theology of the Trinity, and eventually to the doctrine of the eternal spiration of the Holy Spirit. Others, rather fancifully one feels – like to think that "carol" originates in the word "Carolus" the Latin for "Charles" and that because as a song form it became so extraordinarily popular during the reign of Charles I (1600-1649) it took its name from its royal patron. This is not likely, for carols are a mediaeval product and were in use many years before his time. Finally, there is the opinion put forward by Percy Dearmer in the preface to the *Oxford Book of Carols* where he maintains that the word "carol" is derived through the old French "caroler" and the Latin "choraula" from the Greek "choraules" meaning a flute-player for chorus-dancing, and eventually from "choros" signifying a dance performed in a circle.[4] This seems to be the most likely explanation and it is the one mostly favoured by scholars of the present day. So Bramley was right after all.

Etymology however does not take us very far, and if we would satisfy our enquirer there is nothing for it but to define the term. Rimbault dismisses the carol as merely – "a song of devotion", and Eric Blom gives a definition that is equally unsatisfactory – "a Christmas song dating from the fourteenth and fifteen centuries in England, but older on the Continent".[5] Percy Scholes' definition is fuller and better – "a carol is a religious seasonal song of joyful character in the vernacular and sung by the common people".[6] It need hardly be said that anything Cecil Sharp has to say on the subject must involuntarily command the greatest respect. He does in fact in his *English Folk-Song* make the observation that "the carol stands midway between the hymn and the ballad, and may be regarded with equal propriety as a secular hymn or a sacred ballad".[7] Yet it is Percy Dearmer's definition that is the best known – "carols are songs with a religious impulse that are simple, hilarious, popular, and modern"; by "modern" we are to understand as Erik Routley points out – "set in such language as shall express the manner in which the ordinary man at his best understands the ideas of his age, and bring the traditional conservative religion up to date".[8] What reply, therefore, are we to make to our questioner when pressed for an answer? We could not do better than reply in the words of Richard Leighton Greene of Harvard University: "A carol is a song on any subject composed of uniform stanzas and provided with a burden."[9] It is in this sense that the term is understood by Manfred Bukofzer, Gustave Reese, and Frank Harrison, and it is in the same sense that the term is used in the following pages.

As a song form the carol is unique. The stanza-burden design of the carol is nothing unusual; it is a universal pattern common to many types of song sacred and secular alike, but the unique character of its literature sets it apart from all other types of song and places it in a class of its own. The carol can only be described as something specifically English. In the Introduction to his *Early English Christmas Carols* Professor Robbins begins by admitting that the very title of his book is tautological in that the carol is found only in the mediaeval period between 1425 and 1550 and is restricted to England. He is supported in his opinion by no less a scholar than Manfred Bukofzer who writes: "Although the carol developed concurrently and probably in connection with such continental strophic forms as the virilai and the lauda, it must be regarded as specifically English, even if several continental cantilenas have the same form and the same musical style."[10] Richard Leighton Greene in the Introduction to his *Early English Carol* quotes from among some Franciscan sermon notes the very earliest of all our Christmas carols written at some time previous to 1350:

STANZA: A child is boren amonges man
And in that child was no wam
That child ys God, that child ys man
And in that child oure lif bygan.

BURDEN: Honnd by honnd we schulle ous take
And joye and blisse schulle we make
For the deuel of elle man haght forsake
And Godes Sone ys maked oure make.[11]

The carol is distinguishable from other popular song forms by certain unmistakable characteristics. For instance, it is distinct from the hymn; for while the hymn praises God directly and addresses Him in Person, the carol does so indirectly through picturesque references to such inessentials as – the beasts of the manger, the stars, the shepherds and the angels. In this way it differs radically from the religious songs of Saint Francis and his followers. Its extrovert and uninhibited approach to the worship of God is the outcome of the salutary influence of the liturgy in an age when religion was integrated with national culture and the English way of life, and when the official ceremonial of the Church took first place. The hymn on the other hand is an alien imposition, and reflects a private spirituality of a later age. It derives from the puritan psalm-tunes of the Church of John Calvin (1509-1564) and both from the literary and musical point of view, has, particularly in its influence on devotional hymnology – accounted for some of the ugliest features of the counter Reformation.

A carol is not a ballad. A ballad is a narrative poem that tells a story simply and crisply and there makes an end. It comes to the point straightway; its objectivity – its matter of fact and almost curt approach to the subject in hand is one of the hallmarks of the ballad. The carol on the contrary is known and loved precisely for its tenderness and fondness for poetic imagery and symbolism. The ballad moreover is the outcome of a sustained oral transmission; the carol has come down to us through the written record and is found preserved in pocket manuscripts, chap-books, broadsides and garlands. The carol therefore – unless it is a folk-song, is not a communal product rounded and perfected by that corrupting process upon which the very creation of the folk-product depends, but is preserved as in a cocoon, leading a static existence in manuscript form. Finally, and most important of all – the burden of the carol is completely independent of the stanza, whereas the refrain of the ballad is interlarded between the lines of the verses as in the Newcastle ballad "I Saw Three Ships". As a dance, therefore, the rhythm of the ballad would not be as continuous or as smooth as that of the carol.

NOËL

(by Hilaire Belloc 1870-1953)

On a winter's night long time ago,
(The bells ring loud and the bells ring low),
When high howled wind and down fell snow,
(Carillon, carillon, carilla).
Saint Joseph he and Nostre Dame,
Riding on an ass, full weary came
From Nazareth into Bethlehem.
And the small child Jesus smile on you.

At Bethlehem inn they stood before
(The bells ring less and the bells ring more)
The landlord bade them begone from his door
(Carillon, carillon, carilla).
"Poor folk", says he, "must lie where they may,
For the Duke of Jewry comes this way
With all his train on a Christmas Day".
And the small child Jesus smile on you.

Poor folk that may my carol hear
(The bells ring single, and the bells ring clear)
See God's own son had hardest cheer!
(Carillon, carillon, carilla).

Men grown hard on a Christmas morn:
The dumb beast by and a babe forlorn.
It was very, very cold when our Lord was born.
And the small child Jesus smile on you.

Now these were Jews as Jews must be
(The bells ring merry and the bells ring free)
But Christian men in a band are we
(Carillon, carillon, carilla).
Empty we go, and ill bedight,
Singing Noël on a Winter's night:
Give us to sup by the warm firelight,
And the small child Jesus smile on you.

There is no connection whatsoever between the carol and the noël, and it is a common mistake to use the two terms indiscriminately. During the fourteenth and fifteenth centuries when the carol was flourishing in England, the noël was almost unknown, and it was only towards the end of the sixteenth century when the formation of our carol repertory was almost complete that it began to make its appearance in Europe on any large scale. Jean Tisserand (d. 1494) whom Gastoué calls "Le vrai fondateur du cantique populaire" is the first known author of the French noël, and many of his songs are sung on the Continent even today.

The noël is not a carol but a Christmas song concerned exclusively with the Nativity. A noël for Passiontide is therefore a contradiction in terms, but a carol for Passiontide such as "All in the Morning" is perfectly normal. The carol and the noël therefore are poles apart: the carol is a dance-song whereas the noël has no necessary connection with the dance at all. The carol has a definite metrical form; the noël may have any verse form the composer cares to choose. It is essential to the carol that it be formed of uniform stanzas, and that in performance the burden be sung first by the crowd and repeated after the singing of each stanza by the soloist; the noël on the other hand may or may not have a burden as the poet thinks fit, and the verses may vary considerably from very long to very short. "Noël" a contraction of "Le jour de Noël" is derived from the Latin "dies natalis" meaning birthday, and in our carol burdens it appears not as a noun synonymous with Christmas but as an interjection or exclamation of joy. In effect it is the equivalent of "whoopee" or "hip hip hurrah" with all the jollity and abandon that it implies. Its usage therefore is not necessarily restricted to the Christmas season, and the burden "Noël" is frequently found in carols such as "The Mortality Carol" that have no connection with Christmas at all.

Before we proceed any further on the subject of the English carol, we should I think take a quick look at the history of the stanza-burden song form, for its roots go back a very long way into history – even to pre-Christian times. The earliest examples are found in the music of the synagogue: in a "sequence of psalms" or "sacred song-cycle" sung in every Jewish household on the night of the Passover, a psalm was sung by the head of the house to which the rest of the family answered after each verse – "Hallelu – Jah". Yet another early example – this time from the Apostolic age is the "Ubi Caritas" in which we still have with us today both music and text as it was sung at the Agape or "Love Feast" in the second century. The "Gloria Laus" from the liturgy of Palm Sunday – one of the most loved chants in the Gallican Ritual before the days of the Carolingian Empire, and the "Lumen ad revelationem Gentium" from the feast of the Purification are other early examples of the stanza-burden song form. The "O filii et filiae" of Eastertide may be passed over as being so well known as to require no special observation, but we should not forget the Divine Office where in the course of Psalm 94 at the beginning of Matins the Invitatorium "Venite adoremus" is repeated by the entire monastic community after the recitation of each of the six verses by the cantor or soloist. We give here the Advent song that has been in use in Western Christendom for centuries; it is taken from the Introit of the Mass for the Fourth Sunday of Advent:

BURDEN: Rorate coeli desuper, et nubes pluant
justum.

STANZA: Ne irascaris Domine, ne ultra memineris iniquitatis: ecce civitas Sancti facta est deserta: Sion deserta facta est: Jerusalem deserlata est: domus sanctificationis tuae et gloriae tuae, ubi laudaverunt te patres nostri.

BURDEN: Rorate coeli . . .

STANZA: Peccavimus, et facti sumus tamquam immundus nos, et cecidimus quasi folium universi: et iniquitates nostrae quasi ventus abstulerunt nos: abscondisti faciem tuam a nobis, et allisisti nos in manu iniquitatis nostrae.

BURDEN: Rorate coeli . . .

STANZA: Vide Domine afflictionem populi tui, et mitte quem missurus es: emitte Agnum dominatorem terrae, de petra deserti ad montem filiae Sion: ut auferat ipse jugum captivitatis nostrae.

BURDEN: Rorate coeli . . .

STANZA: Consolamini, consolamini popule meus: cito veniet salus tua: quare moerore consumeris, quia innovavit te dolor? Salvabo te, noli timere, ego enim sum Dominus Deus tuus, Sanctus Israel, Redemptor tuus.

BURDEN: Rorate Coeli desuper, et nubes pluant[12] justum.

(*English translation of the Advent song*: "Rorate coeli")

BURDEN: Drop down dew, ye heavens, from above, and let the clouds rain down the Just One.

(cf. Chap. 3, p. 83, for the use of "dew" in connection with the fertility theme in the "lingua franca" of folk-song.)

STANZA: Be not angry, O Lord, and remember no longer our iniquity: behold the city of Thy Holy One has become a desert: Sion is become a desert: Jerusalem is desolate: the house of Thy sanctification and Thy glory, where our Fathers praised Thee.

We have sinned and are become as one that is unclean: and we have all fallen as a leaf, and our iniquities like the wind have carried us away: Thou hast hidden Thy face from us, and hast crushed us in the hold of our iniquity.

Behold, O Lord, the affliction of Thy people, and send forth Him who is to come: send forth the Lamb, the ruler of the earth, from the rock of the desert, to the mount of the daughter of Sion: that He may take away the yoke of our iniquity.

Be comforted, be comforted, my people: thy salvation cometh quickly: why art thou consumed with grief? for sorrow hath estranged thee: I shall save thee; fear not, for I am the Lord thy God, the Holy One of Israel, thy Redeemer.

When dealing with mediaeval music it is of the utmost importance to bear in mind what Wilfred Mellers is at pains to emphasize – that in pre-Reformation England as indeed throughout Europe generally, to be a composer meant in effect to be a composer of sacred and liturgical music. A fifteenth-century composer of the stature of a John Dunstable (d. 1453) would as a matter of course devote his energies primarily to the adornment of the Sarum Ritual in the service of the Church. Secular and extra-liturgical compositions such as the polyphonic carol were of secondary consideration, and when they did appear they were invariably in the same style and of the same texture as the Masses and motets of the period. This was inevitable, for the Church was the poor man's library and the foremost concert hall of the epoch:

> Since the composer was the servant of the Church, to be a writer of music was inevitably to be a writer of liturgical music. In essentials the beliefs of the Church were accepted alike by the most powerful intellects and by those more or less incapable of thought. Therefore there could be no clear distinction between music that was written for liturgical purposes and that which was written for other purposes. This is why the technique of the secular madrigal differed in degree rather than in kind

from the technique of the religious motet.[13]

The importance of this fact alone will be readily appreciated when we consider the music of the troubadours whose minstrelsy had such a lasting influence on European song for more than two centuries.

The troubadours were a society of minstrels who flourished roughly from the end of the eleventh century to the beginning of the fourteenth. The troubadour was usually a cultured gentleman of aristocratic or princely birth, who – inspired by the social, religious, or political world of his day – wrote his own poems and sung them to music of his own composing to the accompaniment of a stringed instrument which he played himself. The word "troubadour" is derived from the Provençal "trobar" and "trobador" through the Latin "tropus" and ultimately from the Greek meaning an ornament, or in the language of musical grammar a "turn".[14] The word "trope" was originally used to designate a florid form of ornamental chant which first appeared in the eighth or ninth century.[15] The troubadours inhabited the wine country of southern France – particularly the regions of Languedoc and Provence and the lowlands of Le Tour de Carol at the foot of the Pyrenees. The earliest of the mistrels was Guilhem IX, seventh count of Poitiers and ninth duke of Aquitaine; other celebrities were Marcabru of Gascony (d. 1147) who fulfilled the double rôle of troubadour and woman-hater – a most strange combination when we reflect that the love-poets were the harbingers of the Age of Chivalry, and Bernart de Ventadorn (d. 1195) son of a kitchen scullion and the finest poet of them all.[16] The religious songs belong to the end of the thirteenth century and in the main were the work of Guiraut Riquier and the "moine-trouvère" – Gautier de Coinci (d. 1236) of the Order of St Benedict. His "Les Miracles de Notre Dame" is a collection of thirty poems each of which is set to an appropriate melody. It is more likely here than anywhere else that we shall find the archetype of our English carol.

France, the eldest daughter of the Church, has always been

recognized as the home of Western Chant; and ever since the days of the Frankonian Choir Schools in the eighth century when the art of free composition known as "troping" had produced the highly ornate plainsong of the Silver Age (850-1100) that was to have so great an influence on the "organa" of Leonin (*c.* 1170) and the "clausulae" of Perotin (*c.* 1183), the liturgical music of Western Christendom has always had a most profound influence on both secular and sacred song. This influence has overflowed even into the field of keyboard music, and any ordinary music-lover who has attended the lunch-time organ recitals given in our big cities will have observed for himself how radically the official music of the Church has moulded the compositions of such as Widor, Vierne, and Guilmant, and inspired the art of improvisation or "troping" in such exponents as Marcel Dupré and Jean Demessieux. Even in our own age, the music of French composers is scarcely ever free from the influence of its Gregorian heritage.

A brief examination of troubadour songs will quickly reveal how closely their forms resemble the song forms in Western Chant. For instance, most troubadour songs cater for soloist and general assembly. The "chanson de geste", an epic poem of great length made up of "tirades" or unequal verses, and modelled on the Latin litany – ends with a coda or tailpiece which is repeated as an afterthought either on the lyre or as a chorus for the audience, with the very practical advantage of allowing the minstrel to take a rest and to recover his breath. Both the "strophic laisse" and the "chanson avec des refrains" also provide for solo and chorus, but it is the "retrouange" that approaches nearest to the form of our English carol. This is a dance-song in stanza-burden form, each stanza ending with a "rounding" or cue that gives the signal to the audience to be ready to enter with the burden. The troubadour was a good psychologist and he took good care to see to it that the "rounding" was identical with the beginning of the burden; in this way the penny never failed to drop. Other troubadour forms influenced by the liturgy were the "lai" and the "estampie" both of which are obvious imitations of the Sequence of the Mass.

Finally, and most important of all: among the rondel forms all of which have at least one refrain – some as many as two or three, it is noticeable that as the song develops and its form begins to crystallize, the tendency is to make the refrain independent of the other units of the stanza.

In the years preceding the birth of Saint Francis, troubadour influence in northern Italy had been pronounced, and therefore is of paramount importance when dealing with the origin and development of vernacular and religious song. In the twelfth and thirteenth centuries a brisk trade was in progress between Italy and France, and cloth merchants from Umbria would be abroad with their bales of merchandise for months at a time in search of a good market for their silks and velvets among the pleasure-loving peoples of Languedoc and Provence. Commercial agents from Genoa and Jewish speculators from Lombardy were constantly abroad, and some had even made as far as London in the interests of commerce and international finance. Keen barter between England and Aquitaine existed at this period, and Robert le Chaucer grandfather of the poet held a key position at the Customs Office where he supervised the importing of wines from the Continent. Geoffrey Chaucer (1340-1400) who came from a line of prosperous vintners very soon discovered that the family name had involved him in diplomatic affairs of state which took him abroad on secret business.[17] It was in 1372 that he made his first visit to Genoa to negotiate with two merchants on the use of an English port for the facilitating of Genoese trade. Admittedly the troubadours as a society were on the wane at the time of Chaucer, but his comings and goings do indicate a trade relationship between Italy and Europe that had been in existence for a very long time. In fine, the continual commercial intercourse between northern Italy and the Continent was the channel by which troubadour culture passed from Provence to northern Italy just as centuries before Christianity had travelled to Britain by the transport made available by the Roman army.

We ought not therefore to be surprised to find the Tuscany and Umbria of the twelfth and thirteenth century on the way to becoming a troubadour colony. Troubadours such as Reimbautz de Vaquieras, Peire Vidal (d. 1215), and Gaucelm Faidit were almost as much at home in Italy as they had been in Languedoc. The people of northern Italy spoke a form of French, and for a long time it was uncertain whether the French of Provence or some other dialect of southern France would prevail and spread southwards to become the national language of Italy. It was Dante (1265-1321) the father of the Italian language who settled the issue by turning his Tuscan into Italian as in later years Chaucer was to turn his Norman-French into English. It was from the minstrel Arnaut Daniel (d. 1199) that Dante copied the form of the "sestina", and Sordello (1180-1270) to whose memory Robert Browning in 1840 devoted an entire poem – is frequently mentioned by Dante in his "Purgatorio". It was on literary form that troubadour influence first exerted itself, and it was here that the Provençal "ballada" shaped the Italian "ballata" which more closely than any other form resembles the English carol.

The forerunner and nearest approach to our English carol is the Italian "ballata", a popular dance in stanza-burden form, and it was upon this that the Flagellants of northern Italy modelled their "Laude Spirituali".[18] These were penitential songs sung in the course of a ritual that was intended to atone for the sins of the past and implore the mercy of God. The lay fraternities that sponsored this type of exhibitionism were in existence early in the eleventh century, but the revival of the movement in 1260 was due to the impetus it received as a result of plague and pestilence and the devastation that followed upon the bloody wars between Frederick II and the Papacy. The "Laude Spirituali" were sung during a public religious procession. When the procession was at a standstill during the singing of the stanza[19] by a precentor the participants would scourge themselves; the flagellations would cease for the singing of the burden when the procession continued on its way. A fourteenth century manuscript preserved at Florence contains no less than a hundred of these songs, and forty-six other specimens may be found in a thirteenth-century document at

Cortona. The songs are modal in character and afford yet another example of the influence of Gregorian Chant on popular song. As in the English carol the burden which is independent of the verse is repeated after each stanza, but occasionally it is sung only at the end, or at the beginning and end of the song, and the "rounding" is a truncated version of the chorus. It was upon these songs that the friars based their vernacular hymns.

During the eleventh and twelfth centuries, Manicheism, a heresy denying the Incarnation, was prevalent in Italy, and it was to combat this evil that St Francis of Assisi (1181-1226) introduced the crib in 1223. St Francis is known as the parent of the carol, and not without reason for he popularized a type of devotional song in the vernacular modelled on the religious songs of the period. Father Cuthbert, O.S.F.C., is only saying what is now generally accepted when he writes: "There can be little doubt that the singing of hymns in the vernacular owed its popularity if not its origin, at least in Italy, to the friars."[20] They would write a religious and devotional poem and unite it to a well-known and popular tune so that the peasants singing the verses – if only for the sake of the tune, would eventually come to a greater knowledge of their Christian religion. It was with this end in view that the lullabies were purposely composed, and the people would come with their torches and bagpipes to sing and dance these simple songs before the crib erected in his hermitage at Grecchio. The charming Gallician song "Torches" might easily have been in use among the Neapolitans at a later date, and found its way to Spain to reappear in the version of Pérez Ballesteros.

TORCHES

(tr. J. B. Trend)

Torches, torches, run with torches
All the way to Bethlehem!
Christ is born and now lies sleeping;
Come and sing your songs to him!

Ah, Ro-ro, Ro-ro, my baby,
Ah, Ro-ro, my love, Ro-ro;

Sleep you well, my heart's own darling,
While we sing you our Ro-ro.

Sing, my friends, and make you merry,
Joy and mirth and joy again;
Lo, he lives, the King of heaven,
Now and evermore, Amen.

Jacaponi da Todi (d. 1306) one of the claimants to the authorship of the Stabat Mater and the greatest of all composers of "laude", wrote in all one hundred and two songs of which ninety-two are in stanza-burden form.

It is only fitting that we should know something of the personality of the swashbuckling character who as minstrel was to have such a profound influence on popular song, and as troubadour-ascetic was to experience the heights of mysticism. His father Pietro Bernardone was a prosperous Umbrian salesman – adventurous, imaginative, and with a quick turn of speech indispensable in one who lived by his wits, and the success of whose ventures depended upon first impressions. He had made his wealth in the south of France where there had been a good market for his embroideries, and two or three times each year he would make the journey from Tuscany to Herault in a bid to sell his wares in the land of the troubadours. It was on such an occasion when away from home that his son was born. His mother christened him "John", but his father, who had lost his heart to the French way of life had the child renamed "Frank" or "Francis" upon his return. The boy grew up to become even more of a troubadour than his father, and "the little Frenchman" as he came to be called, or "Frenchy" as he would have been nicknamed at school today – developed into a typically gay and chivalrous troubadour speaking the language of the love-poets of Languedoc, and revelling like a courtier in all the refinement of an elegant society. G. K. Chesterton in his short biography of the Saint describes the charming personality of the young man in a few well-chosen lines:

> He was the morning star of the Renaissance. Francis was one of those people who are popular with anybody in any case; and his guileless swagger as a troubadour and leader of French fashions made him a sort of romantic ringleader among the young men in the town. He had the love of gay and bright apparel which was inherent in the heraldic taste of mediaeval times and seems altogether to have been rather a festive figure. If there was one thing of which so humble a man could be said to be proud it was his good manners. He was the first hero of humanism.[21]

Seen through English eyes and from the standpoint of our English way of life, our concept of St Francis must inevitably be of an English St Francis whereas as we all know perfectly well – he was an Italian. Yet strange though it may sound, in the twelfth century he would have been considered far more English than Italian precisely because he was so European. This then was the father of the carol: the man who as founder of the Order of Friars Minor was to popularize the crib and the tableau, and give the impetus to a movement from which all modern vernacular hymn singing takes its rise. Dr Greene in his *Early English Carol* gives a very fair assessment of the early Franciscan vernacular movement: "The tradition of vernacular religious songs was begun by St Francis himself. Neither the religious fervour nor the popular sacred poetry of the thirteenth century was initiated by Francis, but the founding of the Order of Friars Minor in 1209 gave an impetus to the movement."[22]

Known as "Les jongleurs de Dieu" or "God's tumblers" the genial compositions of Saint Francis and his followers took the form of simple professions of Christian faith that were all the more Christian for being so jolly. In Dr Greene's own words: "The mildly spectacular character of the friars' ways was one of the secrets of their mighty influence with people who had become indifferent to the routine religion of their parish church."[23] It was just after St Francis had composed "The Song of Brother Sun" that he gave to his disciples the charge of sacred minstrelsy: "What are the servants of God if not his minstrels who ought to stir and incite the hearts of men to spiritual joy?"[24] He was the most Christian of Saints. Even amid the rigours of his penitential exercises he was ever the most cheerful of men, and to the people of his day the most noticeable feature of his personality was that in spite of the severity of his mortifications, no man alive was so full of the joy of living, so gentlemanly, so much in touch with his fellows, and so chivalrous and attentive in all his encounters with the fair sex. G. K. Chesterton has once again left us a pen-picture of this saintly courtier:

> He was a troubadour of a newer and nobler romance; he was to the last agonies of asceticism a troubadour. He was a lover. He was a lover of God, and he was really and truly a lover of men – possibly a much rarer mystical vocation. The reader cannot even begin to see the sense of a story that may well seem to him a very wild one until he understands that to this great mystic his religion was not a thing like a theory, but a thing like a love affair.[25]

His love for his fellow-men was unbounded. Folk-song is the common inheritance of humanity; it is an international possession and the voice of humanity itself. It is no common coincidence therefore that the name of St Francis should be so closely connected with the history of the folk-carol when we reflect that it is in the repertory of folk-carols that the finest specimens of folk-song are to be found. This was the man, and this the spirituality that was the mainspring of the Christmas carol; the song that the common people have made their own and the popularity of which has never been diminished. In its earliest beginnings it was inspired by the greatest mystic the

Church has ever produced. It is a product of the bright and genial spirituality of the Franciscan friary.

In 1224 the first Franciscans landed in England where they soon began to attract the same following as in Italy and on the Continent. They were not slow to divine the spiritual needs of the people and saw at once in the use of simple religious songs in the vernacular an effective means of instructing them.[26] The technique was the same: a simple symposium of Christian theology in the form of a poem set to an attractive tune. These religious songs had the same pastoral value as centuries before, stained glass had had in the hands of the Benedictines. The Church had always been the poor man's library, and as simple folk had previously learnt their religion from the great windows of the cathedral as from a picture-book, so did they now grow in the knowledge of their Christian faith through the songs of the friars. The friars were mendicants in imitation of the example of their founder; they lived out of doors, and their songs were intended originally for out-door use – on the village green, or before the crib in the market square. They did not write for the collegiate church or the cathedral choir but for the ordinary people, and it is for this reason that so many of their songs have been discovered in pocket manuscripts and chap-books that had once been the possession of simple people who used them for the purpose of private devotion and spiritual reading.

By far the greater proportion of our English carols are of a religious and moralistic nature – Professor Robbins puts it as high as eighty per cent, Gustave Reese a little higher – at eighty-three and a third per cent or five out of every six. Thomas of Hale was the earliest of English carol writers but the most prolific was James Ryman, and in a manuscript of 1492 one hundred and sixty-six carol texts are attributed to him alone – one quarter of our entire carol literature earlier than 1550. Of these one hundred and nineteen are in stanza-burden form.

On the subject of the mediaeval carol Dr Greene makes the following observation: "The English religious carol stands removed from true folk-song by one more degree than does the carol genre as a whole; it is a pious imitation of secular song which is itself a development from folk-song."[27] Whether we agree or disagree with his statement, the fact remains – as a glance at the *Guide to English Folk Song Collections* by Margaret Dean-Smith will clearly show – that today a large number of our Christmas carols are in fact accepted as folk-songs by leading ethnomusicologists and students of folk-song. No less an authority than Cecil Sharp himself says outright: "Musically regarded, the traditional carol is not to be distinguished from the folk-song,"[28] and indeed the broadside carol was often directed to be sung to some well-known folk-tune. Moreover, there are several genuine folk-songs such as "Nowelle Nowelle", "God Rest You Merry, Gentlemen", "The Withy Carol", "The White Paternoster" – some of them of supreme literary and musical beauty that have been gleaned from the English countryside within living memory, even if as Sharp says himself – they are fast disappearing.

In his *Early English Christmas Carols* first published in London in 1961 Professor Hope Robbins suggests the theory that the English carol derives not from the Italian "ballata" through the "Laude Spirituali" and the songs of the friars, but directly from the processional hymns of the Sarum liturgy of the English Church of the fifteenth century. This contention he applies both to monophonic and polyphonic carols, and his collection contains thirty beautiful specimens from the early fifteenth century, twenty-three of which are culled from the greater and lesser manuscripts of the same period: the Trinity College MS, the Bodleian MS, the Egerton MS, the Ritson MS, and documents to be found preserved in the British Museum, the Bodleian Library, and the Universities of Cambridge and Glasgow.[29]

Professor Robbins loses no time and says at the outset: "Rather than account for some eighty per cent of all the carols being religious by considering them like the Italian 'Laude' – spiritual parodies or dance songs, it would seem simpler and more logical to look for the origin of these vernacular hymns in the practices of the Church itself." He points out that in the manuscripts the carol is found side by side with the Latin hymn and the antiphon without any attempt on the part of the compiler to discriminate between the liturgical and the non-liturgical, or to show preferment to the Latin over the vernacular; and that in one particular manuscript – the Selden MS, Latin carols or cantilenae mix freely with carols in the vernacular which would seem to indicate that the two were used indiscriminately; otherwise they would have been arranged in separate catalogues for the sake of convenience, and with an eye to everyday practice. Moreover, says the Professor – "there are the annotations and marginal directions that oblige the chorister to 'pray' – 'sing' – 'kneel', and the copious 'prayer tags' and short prayers – all of which are found alongside the vernacular carols, seeming to show that they were employed conjointly with the Latin in the official worship of the Church". He strengthens his contention with the reminder that the stanza-burden form which is the hall-mark of the carol, is precisely that used for the Latin hymn sung in the liturgical procession.

John Stephens, Manfred Bukofzer, and Egon Wellesz all subscribe to this view and Alec Robertson voices his agreement in so many words: "In church and out of church the carol was associated with physical movement; when it was not danced to, it was processed to."[30] Frank Harrison on the other hand is in disagreement: "The theory that carols were sung in ritual processions is untenable, since the ordinals laid down the chants to be sung for processions throughout the year."[31] The whole question is therefore still very much an open one; but what is perfectly clear is that the polyphonic manuscript carols were sung at liturgical services side by side with the official Gregorian Chant by professional choirs, in the Chapels Royal and Collegiate churches in fifteenth century England.

In the preface to his *Early English Christmas Carols* the Professor surprises us with the statement that "most of the English carols commemorate Christmas Day; there are none at all for Easter, Ascension, and Trinity Sunday". This is not quite true;

and in view of the Pauline doctrine on the rôle of Easter in Christian theology, it is hardly likely that the friars who wrote their carols for the express purpose of instructing the peasantry would have omitted through an oversight – the very foundation of their Christian religion! Most important of all, we should remember that the spirituality of the English Franciscans was not only a joyous one, but that it was integrated with the national culture and part and parcel of the English way of life. It aimed not only at instructing the ignorant but at attracting the wayward and at advertising the Christian Way of Life. Accordingly, severe doctrines were never preached for their own sake, but always as an afterthought, and in conjunction with the comforting dogmas to which they stood in opposition, and of which they were the privation. So it was that the disagreeable reminder of the possibility of eternal perdition would be interpolated only after the doctrines of the Incarnation, the Redemption, and the Resurrection had been confidently and fully expounded. Most of our carols therefore deal first and foremost with the Infant lying in the Manger, with His Maiden Mother bending over Him, with the star suspended over His cot, with the beasts of the stall and then, one by one, as in the carol "All in the Morning" – the story of Holy Week, the treachery of Judas, the Crowning with Thorns, the Crucifixion, and lastly the Resurrection. "The Joys of Mary" is yet another carol revealing the wisdom of Franciscan technique. Here, as Dr Greene acknowledges, we are at the very centre of the spirit of Saint Francis:

> The tempering of the austerity of Christianity by the appeal of tender emotion and personal love of Christ, the invocation of pity for his sorrow in the cradle and suffering on the cross which is particularly to be noted in the lullaby and Crucifixion carols, are part of the legacy of Francis to the centuries that followed his ministry.[32]

The work of the friars was not, alas, always confined to the instruction of the laity; they aimed at raising the spiritual tone among the clergy too whenever there was need. Franciscan technique was no different in the "Red Book of Ossory" – a manuscript containing a collection of cantilenae which expressly states were composed – "ne guttura eorum polluantur cantilenis teatralibus, turpis et secularibus" – "so that the clergy should not pollute their throats by popular, immoral and secular songs".[33] This document which unfortunately contains no music, was the work of the Franciscan Richardde Ledrede bishop of Ossory in Ireland (1317-1360) and was meant to meet the needs of the cathedral clergy and for use at the Christmas season. As in the broadsides, so too here: the secular ditty to which the devotional texts were to be sung was indicated at the head of the poem by a rubric or "timbre" which quoted the opening line of the secular song. The cantilena "Peperit Virgo" was to be sung to the tune of "Maiden in the mor lay". Many of these parodies were in the usual stanza-burden form, for instance – the very first in the anthology has the burden "Verbum caro factum est de Virgine Maria". The carol-sequence that according to Erik Routley did service on the feast of the Annunciation, might well have been written by a friar or even by Ledrede himself, for the carol and the sequence were the two forms the friars found most suitable for their purposes.

Professor Robbins adduces his final argument against traditional opinion when he writes: "Critics have assumed that the English religious carol stems from the dance; the theory is questionable for there is not a single recorded example of an early English dance-song in the pattern of a carol." It is true that no monophonic dance forms have been preserved, but surely this is not surprising when we remember that in the fourteenth century England as a nation did not exist, and till the middle of the thirteenth century, the literary language of our country was Norman French! There are preserved however thirteenth-century dance-songs in two and three-part polyphony in the style of the troubadour estampie, for troubadour influence in the twelfth and thirteenth centuries was very strong at a time when England was not only part of Europe, but almost one nation with France. Not only was Eleanor of Aquitaine a great patron of troubadour minstrelsy, but her son Richard Coeur de Lion was himself a troubadour writing his own lyrics and singing them to his own music, as Professor Westrup points out:

> In the second half of the twelfth century England was part of the Angevin Empire, which included Poitou, Guienne, and Gascony, as a result of Henry 2nd's marriage before his succession, to Eleanor of Aquitaine, the divorced wife of Louis VII of France. The literary language of England was Norman French till the middle of the thirteenth century. In consequence a mere handful of English songs with music survive. Some of the wholly French songs seem to be imitations of liturgical music, for instance the songs attributed to Saint Godric who for sixty years lived as a hermit at Finchale on the Wear, and died in 1170.[34]

It is no exaggeration to say therefore, that just as Geoffrey Chaucer was the father of the English language, so too Saint Joan of Arc was the founder of the English nation; and that the prolonged struggle of the Hundred Years War (1388-1453) was but the attempt of one power to annex the other precisely because they had so much in common. On this very point G. K. Chesterton writes:

> It was partly because England and France were so nearly one nation that the kings struggled so long to make them one kingdom. The Black Prince and Bertrand du Guesclin understood each other much better as enemies than French and Foch could understand each other as allies. Behind all was the great unity of Christendom more than twelve hundred years old which the later insular Englishman has never even heard of. France and England did not unite; and the

great English nation was founded, very largely
by Joan of Arc.[35]

What then of the carol – and how did it develop into something specifically English? We might as well enquire how it was that devotion to the Blessed Virgin became a nation-wide cult of such unprecedented proportions, or how came it about that the Most Noble Order of the Garter was created in her honour on the feast of the Purification, by Edward III in 1349 – and how did England come to be known as "The Dowry of Mary"? The truth of the matter is that the English carol with its tender compassion for the sufferings of Mother and Child, was a product of that chivalry that had been brought to this country early in the eleventh century from the heart of Christendom by the courtly love-poets of southern France.[36] It seems therefore reasonable to conclude that the English carol originates not so much in the stanza-burden form of the liturgy, nor in the songs of the friars, but in the chivalry of the troubadours which fashioned its speech and gave it its character.

CAROL

STANZA: This endris night I saw a sight,
A maid a cradell kepe,
And ever she song and seid among
"Lullay, my child, and slepe."

BURDEN: Lullay, my child, and wepe no more,
Slepe and be now still,
The king of bliss thy fader is
As it was his will.

"I may not slepe, but I may wepe,
I am so wo begone;
Slepe I wold, but I am colde
And clothes have I none."

Me thought I hard, the child answard,
And to his moder he said,

"My moder dere, what do I here,
In cribbe why am I laid?

"I was borne and laid beforne
Bestes, both ox and asse.
My moder mild, I am thy child,
But he my fader was.

"Adam's gilt this man had spilt;
That sin greveth me sore.
Man, for thee here shall I be
Thirty winter and more.

"Dole it is to see, here shall I be
Hanged upon the rode,
With baleis to-bete, my woundes to-wete,
And yeve my fleshe to bote.

"Here shall I be hanged on a tree,
And die as it is skill,
That I have bought lesse will I nought;
It is my fader's will.

"A spere so scharp shall perse my herte,
For dedes that I have done.
Fader of grace, whether thou has
Forgeten thy litell sone?

"Withouten pety here shall aby,
And make my fleshe all blo.
Adam, iwis, this death it is
For thee and many mo."

Line 27 – "Baleis", scourges. 30 – "skill", reason. 38 – "blo", pallid. Thomas Wright of the Percy Society, *Songs and Carols* printed for the first time from fifteenth-century MSS, 1847. *Early English Lyrics*, compiled by Sir Edmund Chambers and Frank Sidgwick, 1907. It is noticeable how, in a typical Chaucerian spirit of chivalry, Eve, as a participant in the Fall of Man, is passed over.

CAROL

STANZA: Lesteneth, lordinges, bothe elde and ying,
How this rose began to springe;
Swich a rose to mine likinge
In all this world ne knowe I none.

BURDEN: Of a rose, a lovely rose,
Of a rose is all mine song.

The aungil cam fro hevene tour,
To grete Mary with gret honour,
And seide sche schuld bere the flour,
That schulde breke the fendes bond.

The flour sprong in heye Bedlem,
That is bothe bright and schene.
The rose is Mary hevene quene;
Out of her bosum the blosme sprong.

The ferste braunche is full of might,
That sprong on Cirstemesse night;
The sterre schon over Bedlem bright,
That is bothe brod and long.

The secunde braunche sprong to helle,
The fendes power down to felle;
Therin might none sowle dwelle.
Blessed be the time the rose sprong!

Line 12 – "Schene", fair. Mediaeval MS. carol, Sloane 2593, Thomas Wright, *Songs and Carols* from fifteenth-century MSS, 1856, "Warton Club" founded to honour Professor Thomas Warton of Oxford (1688-1745), and his two sons: Thomas, the younger (1728-1790), and Joseph, the elder (1722-1800), who was in the forefront of the English Romantic Movement. All three were clergymen; cf. *Early English Lyrics* compiled by Sir Edmund Chambers and Frank Sidgwick, 1907.

Chapter 2

The Ballad

In the preceding chapter we asked the question: what precisely is a carol? In reply we gave the clear and uncompromising definition as formulated by Dr Leighton Greene. We now ask: what is a ballad? – an even more important question since the ballad and the carol are closely connected. Sir Arthur Quiller-Couch puts the same poser, but Professor William Ker seems quite sure of the answer; "A ballad is an idea, a poetical form, which can take up any matter and does not leave that matter as it was before. A ballad is 'The Milldams of Binnorie' and 'Sir Patrick Spens' and 'The Douglas Tragedy', and 'Childe Maurice', and things of that sort." What a glib and wholly unsatisfactory reply from so eminent an academician! Dr Greene one feels would have made answer somewhat in the following manner: "A ballad is essentially a narrative poem; it tells a tale by the shortest possible route, and there makes an end."[37] Here for instance is a ballad – "The Five Joys of Mary" probably composed in the fourteenth century by some Franciscan friar, and about which we shall have more to say at a later stage:

Mary, for the love of thee
Blithe and glad may we be,
And I shall sing as ye may see,
   Sua quinque gaudia.

The first Joy was sent to thee
When Gabriel greeted thee
And said Hail Mary in chastity,
Officiaris gravida.

The second Joy was full good
When Christ took both flesh and blood
Without sorrow and changing of mood,
Enixa est puerpera.

The third Joy was of great might
When Jesu was on the Rood dight
Dead and buried in all men's sight,
Surrexit die tertia.

The fourth Joy was without aye
When Jesu to Hell took the way
And with him come great array,
Ad coeli palacia.

The fifth Joy was on Holy Thursday,
Unto Heaven He took the way,
God and man, and so He is for aye,
Ascendit super sidera.[38]

However, before we begin to enter upon a study and an analysis of the ballad, we must be sure to have a clear conception of what is meant by "folk-song" because it was through the ballad-form that in the main, folk-song first made its voice heard. How then do we define folk-song? The *New English Dictionary* of 1901 doesn't even mention the term, although in a supplement included in the edition of 1933 it is described as "a song originating from the people". In the *Century Dictionary* of 1889 it is defined as "a song of the people; a song based on a legendary or historical event, or some incident of common life, the words and generally the music of which have originated among the common people, and are extensively used by them". Funk and Wagnall's *Standard Dictionary* is more to the point: "A song or ballad originating and current among the common people, and illustrating the common life with its interests and enthusiasms as derived from legend or story; also a lyric poem on a popular theme in the style of such a ballad." It was left to Cecil Sharp to give us the first satisfactory definition which has been accepted and acclaimed by all students and collectors of folk-song for the last half century: "Folk-song is the song which has been created by the common people, in contradistinction to the song, popular or otherwise, which has been composed by the educated."[39]

It is no exaggeration to say that British folk-music has now been more thoughtfully studied than that of any other nation. A sharp distinction is drawn between popular song and folk-song, a distinction upon which British students insist far more than students abroad.[40] A popular song is the creation of an individual composer, whereas the folk-tune is the product of the joint efforts of a community. It is a communal composition of which some specimen was at some time or other launched into use by an individual. It is handed down by oral tradition, each singer learning his own ditties, twisting and altering them as he thinks best and passing them on to his neighbour until, like a coin in the pocket, rounded by the passage of time, it became the smooth and polished product that it is today. A dozen generations and a thousand repetitions may have gone to the shaping of one folk-tune. The melodies are usually of a much finer quality than the words precisely because education is a more essential factor in the composing of a poem than a tune.

It is a mistake however, to imagine that folk-song is necessarily primitive or archaic, for although as Dr Greene admits – "British folk-song is now rapidly closing its accounts", it is still composed today in unsophisticated communities that have escaped the influence of wireless and television, and in those areas where conditions of life call for self-entertainment. The observations of Beatricè Blackwood on this very subject make interesting reading:

> Here I should perhaps explain that "primitive" does not mean "simple", for many of the societies thus described are highly complex. Neither does it mean inferior. One of the first ideas of which the ethnologist has to rid himself is that the culture of "primitive" peoples is necessarily on a plane below his own. Again, to describe a culture as "primitive" is not to imply that it is at an early or immature stage of development.[41]

Although it has sometimes been known for genuine folk-song to have made its appearance in our large industrial cities, as in the case of "The Chelsea Lavender Song" – probably an infiltration from the countryside, folk-music may be styled the music of the hamlet and art music the music of the town. Folk-song therefore comes out of the soil. It is the poor man's treasury, the music of the peasant and the ploughboy, the voice of a cultured peasantry and a natural aristocracy. It is moreover the music of a nation, and expresses racial characteristics in a very striking way. For instance, there is no confusing the music of Spain with that of England, Ireland, or Russia, for each has a style peculiar to the spirit of its people. In each case there is not only a homogeneity of style, but something in the nature of a national impulse that comes from the soil itself, combined with a well-ordered beauty that is the hall-mark of the cultured composer. We would do well to reflect and to remind ourselves in the words of a modern author:

> Of what it meant to have a popular tradition which both the people and the more sensitive souls whom we call artists could share together as a common inheritance. The Gothic cathedral, as well as a good deal of mediaeval music, proves

> how tenuous was then the distinction between the average human being and the artist. It is dubious how far the improved sanitation and more universal literacy of later times outweighs such cultural reciprocity.[42]

A large proportion of present-day scholars are keenly interested in the resemblance that folk-song bears to Gregorian Chant in that each is found with a very free rhythm and cast in the idiom of the ancient ecclesiastical modes. Like the Plain-chant the music is very intimately wedded to the text, so much so that, as Cecil Sharp found from personal experience, the folk-singer finds it impossible to sing the melody divorced from the words. It is noticeable too that there is in folk-music little suggestion of folk-harmony, and folk-music for instrumental performance is mainly dance music. Although two-thirds of the fifteen hundred tunes collected by Sharp himself are in the major or Ionian mode, a vast number have been gleaned since his day, and well over five thousand English folk-songs have now been accumulated – many of which are found in the Dorian and Mixolydian modes. Among Celtic peoples folk-music is frequently pentatonic as in the familiar example of "Auld Lang Syne"[43]: the melodies are constructed on a five note scale Doh Ray Me Soh Lah, or else Doh Ray Fah Soh Lah, the "pien tones"[44] or half-tone steps being regarded as ornamental and deliberately omitted to avoid any suggestion of the finality inherent in the perfect cadence. Here in this pentatonic music we have in particular the language of exotic peoples – of the Russian and Hungarian peasantry, and of the nations of the East.[45] A considerable portion of our Gregorian repertory is clearly pentatonic, and there is much too that is characterized by a strong pentatonic feeling; a fact that is inclining scholars to believe that the Chant, as it originally existed in its simple form before it had fallen a victim to the tropings of the Silver Age (850-1100), was composed within the framework of the five note scale and had been greatly influenced by national folk-song – particularly that of the East.[46]

"Robin Hood and the Pedlar"

This pentatonic example was discovered by Dr Vaughan Williams; the opening bar is typical of many folk-tunes particularly those of Celtic peoples, and is identical with the intonation of the Gregorian psalm-tone used in the chanting of Psalm 109. (Cf. *Liber Usualis*, 1925, p. 138, Tone 8.) Notice how passing-notes are approached and quitted by leap!

The illustration quoted above is a Hungarian folk-melody; it keeps particularly close to the pentatonic scale in that its material is confined to F, G, B – flat, C, and D. (Cf. Kodály: *A Magyar Népzene*, 1937, p. 32.)

A right understanding of the ballad is essential while discussing the folk-carol, for both the ballad and carol have common roots. The word "ballad" is derived from the Latin and means a dance. It was performed in a circle, and was not only, with the rondeau and virilai, one of the most fashionable forms of entertainment but a dance of singular charm and grace. As a rule it was composed in common measure with a verse repeating form, but by the time of Shakespeare (1564-1616) the dance and the refrain had disappeared altogether and the ballad became known merely as a song for solo voice. In other words, with the arrival of the Renaissance when Christian culture had reached its height, the English country-folk began slowly to take a less active part in public entertainment much in the same way as the worshipper had been ousted by the virtuosi of the ninth and tenth centuries and had ceased to participate actively in the singing of plainsong of the Roman Mass. The wandering minstrel had assumed control, and the peasant had become a passive listener. Strictly speaking, however, the ballad was a dance, and although in the first instance the work of a single composer, it was of communal growth and began with the dramatic singing of a throng of people under a leader. The ringleader or soloist led the ring dance, singing at the same time certain phrases or additaments to which the people replied in the form of a refrain. The ballad poem was always narrative in form and dealt with the historical, the heroic, or the sentimental with an unsophisticated simplicity and unselfconsciousness that one finds only in simple-minded communities where the members, by reason of circumstances, are the sole source of their recreation and amusement. With its first public performance the ballad was taken up and passed from mouth to mouth, from hamlet to hamlet, like a piece of gossip, producing variants till the most interesting example survived and was approved by the community. As Cecil Sharp remarks in his *English Folk-Song*: "The method or oral transmission is not merely one by which the folk-song lives; it is a process by which it grows and by which it is created."[47] The very corrupting influence of oral communication is the actual means of bringing it into being! No two ballad singers ever sang the same ballad in exactly the same way, and so each locality would come to possess its own version of the communal product.

Although the *ballada* made its first appearance in the eleventh century among the troubadours of Languedoc and the trouvères of the north, yet the custom of a solo effort accompanied by a refrain in which all could take part was nothing new, and in fact was a prominent feature of the liturgy in early Christian times when the entire congregation joined in the singing of the antiphon after each successive verse of the psalm. However it was not until a very much later date that the ballad made its firm appearance in England; it was in fact from the fifteenth century, the era of the Mystery Play, that the bulk of our ballad repertory began to appear.

The primitive folk-ballad was the literary product of an unlettered people in the same way that the folk-tune was the work of the unskilled musician. The origin and evolution of the folk-ballad and the folk-song are the same, and they share the same distinctive characteristics. In a ballad a story is told in as few words as possible; it is impersonal, objective, and rapid in its movement. It is marked by a certain monotony due to the same phrases being repeated over and over again, and a redundancy of expression, all of which help to lessen the strain on the memory of the singer. Hackneyed and conventional phrases are found at the beginning and at the end of the ballad; like children, singers find it hard to begin a story, and having told it are unable to bring it gradually to a satisfactory conclusion. So, just as a child might begin a story with "Once upon a time" and end with "and they all lived happily ever after", the peasant would begin: "As I rode out one May morning" or "As it fell out one May morning", and with this foreknowledge as a ruse, a song collector will often revive and assist an indifferent memory. The ballad story is sketched with a few bold phrases and a great deal is left to the imagination of the listener. The peasants like to believe that the story is true, and here again – like children – they live in a Fairyland of their own. "Yes sir, and it is true", is a postscript that is frequently added at the end of a long ballad.[48]

In so far as the folk-ballad is concerned, on the subject of the "refrain" as to whether or not it is a characteristic feature of this type of literary form, there seems to be a very wide divergence of view among scholars. Cecil Sharp says categorically: "There is no feature that is more characteristic of the popular ballad than the refrain. It forms almost the invariable adjunct to the ballad that has any claim to antiquity. There is reason to believe that the primitive ballad was not only communal in authorship but communal in performance also, and that it was danced as well as sung."[49] It has always been the delight of audiences everywhere and at all times, to have a part in any form of community act whether it be social or religious, and we can hardly imagine the simple country-folk remaining aloof throughout the whole of a musical evening and not adding their own quota to the merry-making. Dr Greene on the other hand writes: "If a ballad has a refrain as occasionally they do, it is a different refrain from the carol burden."[50] This eminent scholar seems to be well off target here, for not only the "shanty-chants" popular among merchant seamen but also the "waulking-songs" still to be heard among the cottage workers of the South Country are very often in ballad form with a burden for use by the entire assembly. A group of basket-makers or rag rug-makers would be at work in the kitchen, and without breaking off their employment one worker would begin the narration while after each stanza the entire company would enter with the burden. Surely, there are a great number of ballads with a recurring theme – presumably for communal use; and although in the *Reliques of Ancient English Poetry* both burdens and refrains are rare, yet they are to be found, as in the ballad "Saint George for England" where the verses vary from twenty to thirty lines in length, and in the "Agincourt Song" in which the burden and the refrain both occur with regularity. There is no smoke without fire; and if refrains do occur, however rarely – there must be a reason for it. Sir Arthur Quiller-Couch gives quite a number of ballads with refrains, but he maintains that they are comparatively rare; and not connecting the folk-ballad in any way with the dance, he writes: "But I should like to say that, of the ballads which survive to us, few carry a refrain; they are far fewer than to justify the stress laid on the refrain by those who trace all balladry to communal dancing."[51] We know that for centuries the folk-ballad was communal property – not too long, and sung either at home, or during the summer season out in the open, after the farmers had finished for the day. With the Renaissance the travelling minstrel arrived catering mainly for the great and noble of the stately homes of England. To satisfy his patrons he pieced together several of the small folk-ballads to form long Epics or Romances, and so for a while, the peasant ballad went out of existence. When however, with the arrival of the printing press the educated classes became no longer dependent on the minstrel for their entertainment, he was forced to turn once again to the country-folk, and accordingly broke up the long Romances into smaller pieces to cater for their simple tastes. Not all our folk-ballads suffered at the hands of the minstrel, although it is now generally held that the greater part of our ballad literature belongs to the second period – the fifteenth and sixteenth centuries. The minstrel's aristocratic audience expected to be entertained and would remain aloof from any active participation in the evening's entertainment, particularly as the minstrel himself was revered as a virtuoso and a Master of his art. Would it not therefore be reasonable to suggest that the refrain disappeared precisely at this period? "The Twelve Joys of Mary" is a folk-ballad with a burden, so also is "The Cherry Tree Ballad" in the version discovered by Thomas Miners of Camborne! Could we not stretch a point and say, that very likely, many of our folk-ballads – particularly the religious ones – are in reality folk-carols from which the burden has disappeared?

However opinion may be divided on the subject of the refrain, it is wholly united in affirming that the apocryphal element first introduced by the Franciscan friars is a characteristic ingredient of the folk-ballad. Some of the finest specimens in ballad literature originate among the "folk" inhabiting the region between the Forth and the Tyne, and it is from this area that we have "The Three Kings of Cologne" and its derivative "I Saw Three Ships".

The legend of the Three Crawns or skulls upon which these ballads are based is as follows: The Three Wise Men who had journeyed to pay homage to the Divine Infant were Melchior, an old man, grey-haired and bearded, bearing gifts of gold; Gaspar, young and beardless with his gift of frankincense; and the dark skinned Balthazar with his offering of myrrh. The story has it that three hundred years after their death, the bodies of the Magi were taken to Constantinople by the Empress Helen; later they were transferred by St Eustatius to the church of St Eustorgio in Milan; in 1162 they were finally transported to Cologne Cathedral by the Emperor Frederick Barbarossa in the care of the bishop Renaldus. In the legend the number of ships is three, and out of reverence for the sacred remains one skull was assigned to each ship; but when of a sudden the skulls came to be supplanted first by one personage, then another, the number of ships began to vary and we find two ships for Jesus and Mary, one ship for the Saviour alone, and in the earliest version of all printed by Ritson, there is only one ship for quite a sizeable complement:

> There comes a ship for sailing then
> Saint Michel was the steres-men,
> Saint John sat in the horn; (*stern*)
> Our Lord harped, Our Lady sang
> And all the bells of heaven they rang
> On Christ's Sunday at morn.

There are three texts on the theme of "The Three Kings of Collein" – the version contained in Thomas Wright's *Songs and Carols*; that found in *Notes and Queries* (6th Series, pp. 505-507) which is fuller and more accurate; and the one dating from the reign of Henry VII (1457-1509). This last contains twelve verses in all, of which Anne Gilchrist gives nine:

> There came three Kings from Galilee
> Into Bethlem that fair citie.
> To seek Him that e'er should be
> By right – a
> Lord and King and Knight – a.[52]
>
> As they came forth with their offring
> They met with Herod, that moody King,

This tide – a
An this to them he said – a.

Of whence be ye, you Kinges three?
Of the east as you may see
To worship Him that e'er should be
Lord and King and Knight – a.

They took their leave both old and young
Of Herod that moody King
They went forth with their offering
By light – a
The star that shon so bright – a.

Till they came into the place
Where Jesu and His Mother was
Offered up with great solace
In fere – a
Gold and cense and myrrh – a.

The father of heaven an angel sent
To these three kings that made present
This tide – a
And thus to them he said – a.

My Lord have warned you every one
By Herod King you go not home
For and you do he will you slone (*slay*)
And hurt you wonderly – a.

Forth they went these kinges three
Till they came home to their countrie
Glad and blithe they were all three
Of the sight that they had see
By dene – a
The company was clene – a.

Kneel we now here a-down
Pray we in good devotion
To the king of great renown

Of grace – a
In heaven to have a place – a.[53]

In 1895 a boatman on the Humber heard the "Crawn Version" which was noted by Lewis Davis of Pinner who sent it to Baring-Gould who published it in his *Garland of Country Songs* of the same year.[54] We give the text here, together with the melody as it was heard in 1895:

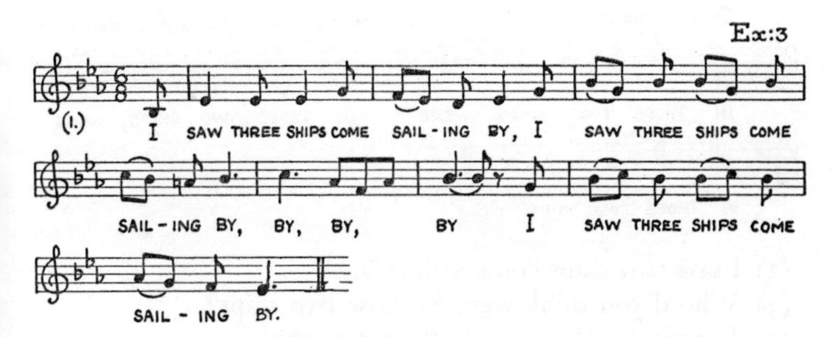
Ex:3
(1.)
I SAW THREE SHIPS COME SAIL-ING BY, I SAW THREE SHIPS COME
SAIL-ING BY, BY, BY, BY I SAW THREE SHIPS COME
SAIL-ING BY.

(2) I axed 'em what they'd got aboard – board – board,
(3) They said they'd got three crawns – crawns – crawns,
(4) I axed 'em where they was taken to – to-o, to-o, to-ooo,
(5) They said they was ganging to Coln upon Rhine, Co-ln, Co-ln,
(6) I axed 'em where they came frae – frae – frae,
(7) They said they came frae Bethlehem – Beth – Beth,

The following version was taken down by Miss Gilchrist at Blackham on the Kent-Sussex border in 1905. She adds that she has heard a variant sung to the text of "London Bridge is Falling Down" with the refrain "My Fair Lady", and remarks that originally it probably read – "Our Fair Lady". Miss Dean-Smith thinks that there is something in this, and writes: "This seems historically justified, since at one time most bridges had a shrine or chapel of a protecting saint incorporated in their structure." It would seem likely therefore that the intercession of the Virgin Mary was sought against the total collapse of the bridge.

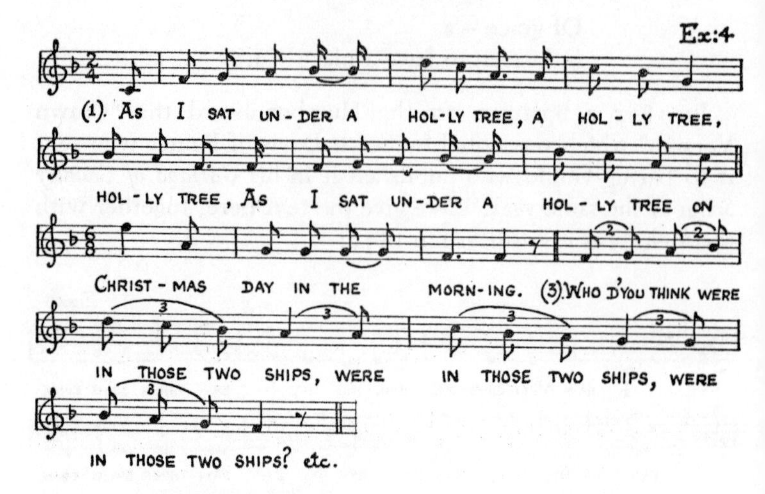
Ex:4
(1). As I sat un - der a hol - ly tree, a hol - ly tree,
hol - ly tree, As I sat un - der a hol - ly tree on
Christ - mas day in the morn - ing. (3). Who d'you think were
in those two ships, were in those two ships, were
in those two ships? etc.

(2) I saw two ships come sailing in,
(3) Who d'you think were in those two ships?
(4) Joseph and Mary was in those two ships,
(5) Where d'you think they were going to?
(6) They were going to Bethlehem,
(7) What d'you think they were going for?
(8) They were going to pay their tax.

The next version which appears under the same title as No. 3 in *The Oxford Book of Carols* but where both music and words are entirely different, was taken down by Anne Gilchrist from some children at Bushey in 1912:

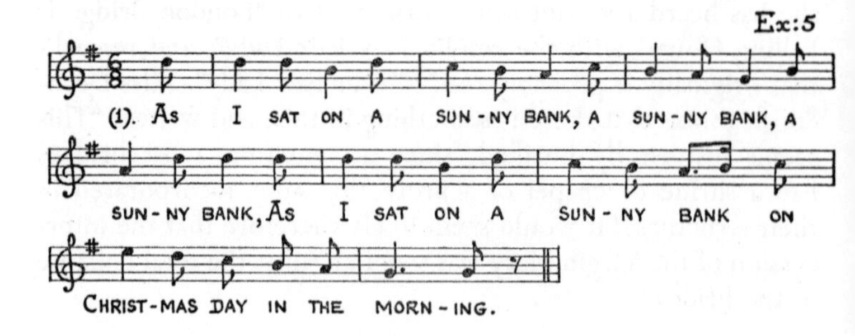
Ex:5
(1). As I sat on a sun - ny bank, a sun - ny bank, a
sun - ny bank, As I sat on a sun - ny bank on
Christ - mas day in the morn - ing.

(2) I saw three ships come sailing by, etc.
(3) I asked them where they were going to,
(4) They said they were going to Bethlehem,
(5) I asked them who they had got in,
(6) They said they had the Saviour.

The following example would seem to suggest that the ballad was sometimes sung as a "Wassail Song" in the course of a "luck-visiting" expedition; the final verse quite clearly calls for some form of remuneration as a reward for the foot-slogging efforts of the songsters:

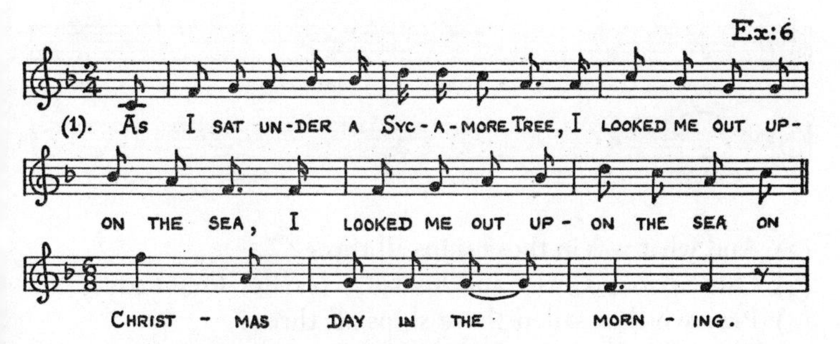

(2) I saw three ships a-sailing there,
The Virgin Mary and Christ they bare;
The Virgin Mary and Christ they bare
On Christmas Day in the morning.

(3) He did whistle and She did sing,
And all the bells on earth did ring;
And all the bells on earth did ring
On Christmas Day in the morning.

(4) And now we hope to taste your cheer
And wish you all a happy new year;
And wish you all a happy new year
On Christmas Day in the morning.

This last example is in the form as it was generally known by the Londoner forty years ago. Its tone is more courteous than that of the earlier versions mentioned, and lacks the inquisitiveness of the north-countryman. It resembles the version found in Sandys' collection of 1833 that is included in *The Oxford Book of Carols* under No. 18:

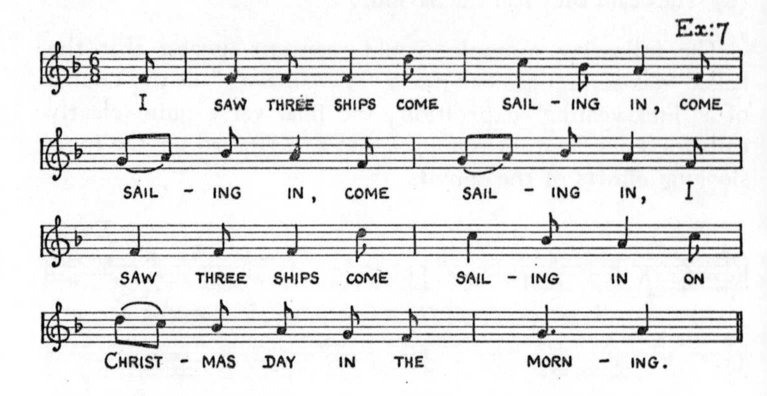
Ex:7
I SAW THREE SHIPS COME SAIL - ING IN, COME
SAIL - ING IN, COME SAIL - ING IN, I
SAW THREE SHIPS COME SAIL - ING IN ON
CHRIST - MAS DAY IN THE MORN - ING.

(2) And what was in those ships all three?
(3) Our Saviour Christ and his lady, (earlier Our Lady?)
(4) Pray whither sailed those ships all three?
(5) They sailed into Bethlehem,
(6) And all the bells on earth shall ring,
(7) And all the angels in heaven shall sing,
(8) And all the souls on earth shall sing,
(9) Then let us all rejoice amain,

One of the most interesting examples of apocryphal legend is to be found in "The Cherry Tree Ballad". The story is from the apocryphal Gospel of the Pseudo-Matthew, and tells how during the flight into Egypt, Joseph, Mary and her Divine Offspring stopped and rested under the shade of a palm tree. When Mary asks Joseph to reach for some of the fruit, Joseph becomes annoyed and testily replies that there are more important things to attend to, and that the water is already very low in the bottles. Whereupon Jesus speaks, and immediately the tree bows down its branches to enable Mary to gather the fruit she requires. Joseph is immediately filled with remorse for his ill-humour and humbly asks Mary's forgiveness. The story has many versions, but throughout them all Joseph is represented by the Humanist composers as being, in spite of his noble calling, very human. In the East he is represented as an old man with a beard, generally very tired and sleepy. In England he is depicted as old and inconsiderate as in the version found in Sandys' collection. In the Coventry Mystery Play, "cherry tree" is substituted for "palm tree", and the episode occurs before the birth of Christ in the course of the journey to Bethlehem to conform to the decree of Caesar. But the finest tune of all is that which found its way to America and was reclaimed by Cecil Sharp in 1917.[55] It was taken down from the singing of a settler in the wastes of the mountains of Southern Appalachia where conditions of life were very much like those in England two hundred years ago. We give the ballad with its tune exactly as it was discovered by the collector:

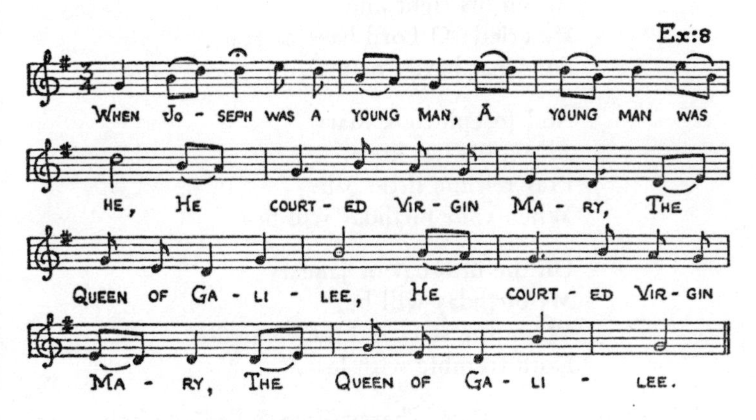
Ex:8
WHEN JO - SEPH WAS A YOUNG MAN, A YOUNG MAN WAS
HE, HE COURT - ED VIR - GIN MA - RY, THE
QUEEN OF GA - LI - LEE, HE COURT - ED VIR - GIN
MA - RY, THE QUEEN OF GA - LI - LEE.

As Joseph and Mary
Were walking one day,
Here is apples and cherries
Enough to behold.

Then Mary spoke to Joseph
So neat and so mild:

Joseph, gather me some cherries,
For I am with child.

Then Joseph flew in angry,
In angry he flew;
Let the father of the baby
Gather cherries for you.

Lord Jesus spoke a few words
All down unto them,
Bow low down, low down, cherry tree,
Let the mother have some.

The cherry tree bowed low down,
Low down to the ground,
And Mary gathered cherries
While Joseph stood around.

Then Joseph took Mary
All on his right knee.
He cried: O Lord have mercy
For what have I done.

And Joseph took Mary
All on his left knee.
Pray tell me little baby
When your birthday will be?

On the fifth day of January
My birthday will be,
When the stars and the elements
Doth tremble with fear.[56]

We cannot leave "The Cherry Tree Ballad" without a reference to the two verses quoted by Francis Child from a version found in the collection of William Sandys. These two stanzas are surely the most poignant and the saddest in the whole of English literature. We need no convincing that Christ was God; perhaps we do not always realize sufficiently that He was truly Man and had all our human emotions in a most refined degree. His being a perfect human nature, He was far more sensitive, and felt far more keenly than the rest of His fellows. There were times when He laughed; there were times when the tears flowed fast and furious. Above all, He loved His Mother and His home, and the thought of the sorrow to His Mother of which He was to be the occasion must have caused His sensitive nature many a bitter pang. It is all there like a cry of anguish, in the last two verses of Sandys' "Cherry Tree Ballad":

> O, I shall be as dead, mother,
> As the stones in the wall;
> O the stones in the street mother,
> Shall mourn for me all.
>
> Upon Easter-Day mother,
> My uprising shall be;
> O the sun and the moon mother,
> Shall both rise with me.

Was it because the mediaeval English peasant dealt so closely with life – caring for it and protecting it in the course of his work on the farm – that he was able to sing with such depth of feeling? There he would be, up at all hours at the lambing season; his weather-eye ever on the expecting heifer, his capable hands ready to receive the young calf. The way in which the word "mother" recurs is so very well timed. The womb is where home begins, and the peasant was alive to this.

Mr H. E. Piggott writing in the *Journal* of the English Folk-Song Society gives a practical illustration of precisely what occurred when the Romances of the fifteenth and sixteenth centuries were broken up into short ballads to meet the needs of the English peasantry. He gives a version of "The Cherry Tree Ballad" discovered by Thomas Miners of Penponds, Camborne, which in the January of 1916 he took down from a Mr Landry of Callington who had previously learnt it from someone he met in Bodmin some years before. Here it is as recorded in the *Journal* of 1916:

BURDEN: Then sing O the holy holy
And sing O the holly
And of all the trees that are in the wood
It is the holly.

STANZA: Then up bespoke Joseph,
With words so unkind,
"Let them pick thee cherries, Mary,
That brought thee with child."

Then whispered Jesus,
So meek in the womb,
"Bow down, gentle cherry bush,
That my mother may have some."

The holly bears a berry
So red as the blood
And Mary bore our sweet Saviour
To do sinners good.

The holly bears a prickle
So sharp as a thorn
And before the next morning
Our sweet Saviour was born.

We shall all be as dead
As a stone in the lane,
And in the next world
We shall all live again.[57]

Thomas Miners added that "the first time Landry sang 'holy, holy, O' or ''oly, 'oly, O'; later he sang ''oly, 'oly, e'. I cannot say whether this is a reference to the great 'O antiphons' of Christmas, but it seems very likely". The Antiphonae Majores are recited in full before and after the Magnificat at Vespers of the Divine Office from the 17th to the 23rd December inclusively. There are seven antiphons in all: "O Sapientia", "O Adonai", "O radix Jesse", "O clavis David", "O Oriens", "O Rex gentium", and finally "O Emmanuel" which we here quote in its entirety:

O Emmanuel, rex et legifer noster
expectatio gentium, et Salvator
earum: veni ad salvandum nos Domine,
Deus noster.

Many of us will be familiar with the ballad beginning "As it fell out one May morning" and recognize it at once as "The Holy Well" given in *The Oxford Book of Carols* as No. 56. Here is a most unusual version of the same ballad under the title "The Bitter Withy", or "Sally Twigs". It was discovered and noted down by the Reverend Edwin King at King's Pyon in 1908: it was sung to him by Mrs Mary Jones sixty years of age.[58] Professor Gummere in *The Popular Ballad* published in 1907 writes that this is the first genuine ballad to have been discovered since the publication of Child's work in 1883:

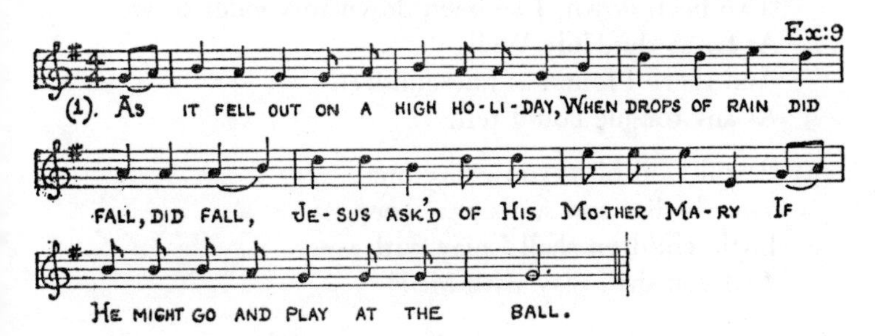
Ex:9
(1). As it fell out on a high ho-li-day, When drops of rain did
fall, did fall, Je-sus ask'd of His Mo-ther Ma-ry If
He might go and play at the ball.

(2) "To play at ball my own dear Son
It's time you're going, or gone,
But let me hear of no complaints
At night when you come home."

(3) Sweet Jesus went down into yonder town
As far as the Holy Well,
And there He saw as fine children
As any tongue can tell.

(4) "I say God bless you every one
Your bodies and souls pray keep,
Little children shall I play with you?
And you shall play with Me."

(5) "Oh nay, oh nay, that must not be,
And oh nay, that must not be,
For we are all lords' and ladies' sons
Born in our bowers all."

(6) . . . . (*wanting*) . . . .
And the very meanest amongst them
Told me I was a poor maid's son
Born in an oxen's stall.

(7) Sweet Jesus turned Himself round about
He did neither laugh nor smile
But the tears ran trickling from his eyes
Like water from the skies.

(8) Sweet Jesus went home to his Mother Mary
"I've been down, I've been down to yonder town
As far as the Holy Well
And there I found as fine children
As any tongue could tell.

(9) "I said God bless you every one
Your bodies and souls pray keep
Little children shall I play with you
And you shall play with Me?"

(10) "Go you down, go you down to yonder town
As far as the Holy Well
And take away those sinful souls
And dip them deep in Hell."

(11) "Oh nay, oh nay, that must not be,
And oh nay, that must not be,
There's many a thousand sinful souls,
Crying out for help of Me."

(12) Jesus made a bridge of the beams of the sun,
And over Jordan went He,
And there followed after the three jolly jordans,
And drowned the three all three.

(13) And its upling corns and downling corns
The mothers of them did whoop and call
"O Mary mild, call home your child,
For ours are drowned all."

(14) Then Mary mild called home her child,
And laid it across her knee
And with a rod of bitter withy
She gave Him thrashes three.

(15) Oh the withy the withy, the bitter withy
Which caused my back to smart!
The withy shall be the very first tree
To perish at the heart.[59]

This ballad is quite obviously a variant of a folk product that began life as a religious poem used by the Franciscans for the instruction of children. There are two apocryphal Gospels of the Infancy upon which the friars may have drawn for their fairy-tales, the first attributed to St James[60] and the second to St Thomas.[61] In each Gospel the Divine Infant appears as rather more than a match for His playmates, and His ability to hold His own invariably makes Him unpopular with His companions who tease Him and act spitefully. Quarrels are incessant: the son of Annas takes a willow switch and spoils Jesus' fish-pools; he is punished for his spite by an attack of paralysis. A boy who jostles Jesus in the street is struck dead, and the son of Hanani is struck down and dies for interfering with the little channels and pools Jesus had made in the sand on the river bank. This may be reflected in the second verse of the poem where Mary tells her son not to bring home the usual tales of woe when He returns in the evening. It is interesting to note that the ballad opens with a shower of rain; it is also raining at the beginning of the first chapter in the Gospel of the Pseudo-Thomas. The stream overflows its banks forming pools of muddy water which Jesus miraculously makes clear again. It is also worth noting that the "Holy Well" mentioned in the tenth verse in the vicinity of which Jesus used to play with His companions, is also referred to in the Gospel of the Psuedo-James. The legend leads us to believe that the Divine Infant was very familiar with the spot, and that on one occasion when His mother sent Him on an errand with the pitcher, the water-pot broke on arriving at the summit; but Jesus miraculously caught the contents in His mantle and arrived home to the great amazement of His Mother.

It is however the twelfth verse that intrigues the student of folk-song, and commenting on "the three jolly jordans" Anne Gilchrist has this to say:

> Has "jerdan" once been the name applied to the pitchers carried by the children in one of the legends from which the carol is derived afterwards misunderstood and applied to the children themselves? According to Halliwell's Dictionary, and Skeat's Dictionary, "jordan" meant a large pot or vessel used by physicians and chemists – like a soda-water bottle with the neck not much smaller than the body of the vessel, but longer than the neck of a soda-water bottle. "Jordan" is short for "jordan-bottle" and there are other forms – "jurdon" and "jordeyne", and connected with it may be "jorum" meaning a bottle, or a beverage.[62]

Professor Gerould quotes three Pseudo-Matthew legends: Zeno's fatal fall, the story of the broken jug, and Jesus sitting on the sunbeam. These are all found in an expanded form in an English fifteenth-century poem at the British Museum. It deals with: the leap from hill to hill fatally imitated by Christ's companions, the repairing of the broken jug, the suspension of the jug on the sun-ray, Jesus sitting on the sunbeam, the story of Zeno, and the gathering up of the spilled water. Two Harleian MSS[63] also tell the same story: Christ's water-pot is hung on the sunbeam and hangs safe and still. His playfellows, not to be outdone try to do the same but their pitchers fall and are broken. Jesus afterwards makes them whole again and the children return home rejoicing.

At Bradwell in Derbyshire an interesting custom throwing light on the subject has persisted down to our own day. On Easter Sunday children were expected to drop a pin into the well; on Easter Monday every child bore throughout the day a bottle filled with sweetmeats. The bottle of any child who had not previously dropped a pin into the well was expected to break, for the fairy who presided over the well was the protector of the bottle.

Here we have one of the most intriguing specimens in the whole of English ballad literature. In the eighth verse, as in the opening stanza of "Sir Patrick Spens", we have an excellent example of that rapidity of movement born of a desire not to weary the audience by taking up too much of their time, which is one of the hall-marks of the genuine folk-ballad. We have also in the penultimate verse a fine example of onomatopoeia – who said that folk-literature was primitive!

We now come to what I believe to be the rarest specimen in English ballad literature – "The Dessexshire Ballad" or "The New Forest Gypsies' Song". I have not found this interesting folk-song in any anthology of Christmas music; it does not appear even in Erik Routley's beautiful edition of *The English Carol* published in 1958. It was discovered by Alice Gillington who received it from a half-gypsy in the south of England, and was included in her *Old English Carols of the Southern Counties* published in 1910. In pre-Reformation times, East Anglia was a catholic stronghold that produced one of the greatest mystics western Christendom has ever known – Saint Juliana of Norwich (1343-1443), and two manuscript copies of her "XVI Revelations of Divine Love" are now happily the treasured possession of the British Museum. It was only inevitable that puritan opposition to traditional Christian culture should have been strongest where the old Faith was the most fervently upheld. The gypsies however were able to preserve their ancient religious beliefs and the culture that went with them, pursuing as they did, an isolated community life apart from normal society, and thereby escaping the rigours of puritan persecution. Even today, East Anglia is markedly puritan in mentality, and we think that this might easily account for the rarity of this particular ballad. So many hamlets in the south of England such as Thorp le Soken bear continental names, and "Dessexshire" is probably a corruption of d'Essexshire where the ballad originated. We give both the words and the music as they were taken down by Miss Gillington "from the mouth of the people":

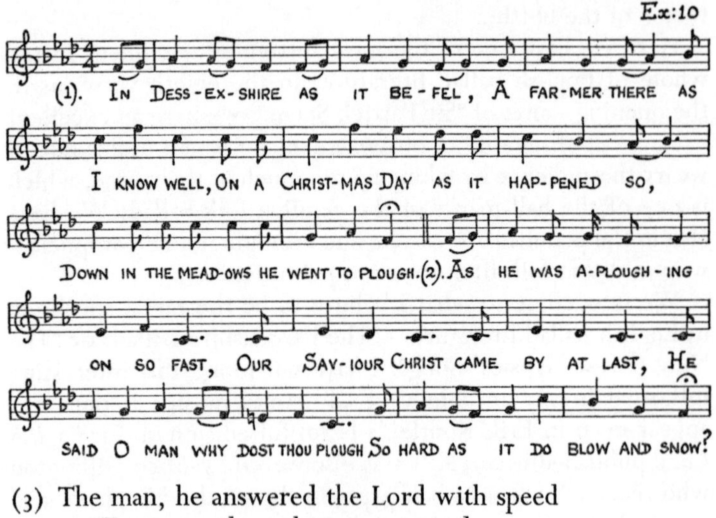
Ex:10
(1). In Dess-ex-shire as it be-fel, A far-mer there as
I know well, On a Christ-mas Day as it hap-pened so,
Down in the mead-ows he went to plough. (2). As he was a-plough-ing
on so fast, Our Sav-iour Christ came by at last, He
said O man why dost thou plough So hard as it do blow and snow?

(3) The man, he answered the Lord with speed
"For to work we have great need
If we wasn't to work all day
We should want some other way."
(4) For his hands did tremble a pass to a fro;
He ran so fast he could not plough;
And the ground did open and let him in,
Before he could repent his sin.
And all the world consum'd at last,
(5) His wife and children were out at play;
And his beasts and cattle all died away,
For breaking of the Lord's Birthday.

In the *Journal* of 1902 (Vol. 1, No. 4) Miss Lucy Broadwood gives us an interesting though much corrupted version of the story of "King Herod and the Cock" and "The Miraculous Harvest" in "The Ballad of King Pharim" or King Pharaoh, taken down in 1893 from three gypsy men of the "Goby" family then residing in Surrey. As we have said earlier many of the traditional ballads that for centuries had been preserved by a sustained oral tradition had fallen a prey to the professional minstrel, and had been strung together to form long Epics or Romances to cater for the aristocratic audiences of an ever growing Renaissance society. At one time therefore ballads such as "The Cherry Tree", "The Carnal and the Crane" or the Crow and the Crane, "King Herod and the Cock", "The Miraculous Harvest", "The Lovely Lion", and "St Stephen and Herod" – were all part of one and the same story of the Infancy of Christ as told in the Apocryphal Gospels and used to such advantage by the preaching friars. The legend of the roasted capon suddenly coming alive, feathering, and crowing, to testify before King Herod to the historical truth of the Incarnation – is an extremely old one and is widely known throughout Europe. Its origin seems to be traceable to two Greek manuscript copies of the pseudo-Gospel of Nicodemus; but there is also an account of the same incident in a MS dating from the time of King Henry VI (1421-1471) and preserved in the British Museum which makes St Stephen the dish-bearer to the King, to silence whose scoffings, and in vindication of his believing servant the capon rises and crows – "Christus natus est". Here then is a new and unusual version of an old story set to a fresh tune and given as it was noted from some gypsy tramps who were very well-known in the neighbourhood of Horsham and Dorking:

Ex:11

KING PHA - RIM SAT A - MUS - ING, A - MUS - ING ALL A -
LONE. THERE CAME A BLES - SED SAV - IOUR, AND ALL TO HIM UN - KNOWN.

"Say, where did you come from, good man,
Oh, where did you then pass?"
"It is out of the land of Egypt,
Between an ox and an ass."

"Oh, if you come out of Egypt, man,
One thing I fain thou know'st
Whether a Blessed Virgin Mary
Sprung from an Holy Ghost?

"For if this is true, good man,
That you've been telling me,
Make that the roasted cock do crow three time
In the place where we did stand."

Oh, it's straight away the cock did fetch
And feathered to your own hand,
Three times a roasted cock did crow,
On the place where they did stand.

Joseph, Jesus, and Mary,
Were travelling for the West,
When Mary grew a-tired,
She might sit down and rest.

They travelled further and further,
The weather being so warm,
Till they came to some husbandman
A-sowing of his corn.

"Come husbandman", cried Jesus,
"Throw all your seed aside,
And carry home your ripened corn.
That you've been sowing this tide.

For to keep your wife and family
From sorrow, grief, and pain,
And keep Christ in your remembrance
Till the time comes round again."

The last ballad of which we shall treat is perhaps the one about which least is known – "The Leaves of Life" or "The Ballad of the Seven Virgins". Mr W. Howitt in his *Rural Life of England* published in 1837 gives a verse of this ballad (Vol. 2, p. 212) that his wife had received from a Miss Jewsbury who had been song-collecting in the Manchester area. The earliest version is that of the *Garland of Christmas Carols* where eleven stanzas of the ballad were published by Joshua Silvester in 1861 – but without a tune. In 1908 two extra verses appeared in Frank Sidgwick's *Popular Carols*; the new verses were discovered in a chap-book of 1847, one of which is to be found appearing word for word in a fifteenth-century lyric, indicating that the ballad is probably one of great antiquity. He also gave a tune which he claimed was the first on record since the days of the puritans. In recent years however, others have been discovered, notably that of 1923 which Cecil Sharp took down from the gypsies of Little Stretton in Shropshire, and the one noted in 1908 by Dr Vaughan Williams from Angelina Whatton, a gypsy living in the neighbourhood of Weobley. The ballad is a most beautiful one, and it is given by Sir Arthur Quiller-Couch – but in a shortened form – in his *Studies in Literature*. We quote it here in its entirety:

All under the leaves, the leaves of life,
I met with virgins seven,
And one of them was Mary mild,
Our Lord's mother from heaven.

"O what are you seeking, you fair maids,
All under the leaves of life?
Come, tell, come tell me what seek you
All under the leaves of life?"

"We're seeking for no leaves Thomas,
But for a friend of thine;
We're seeking for sweet Jesus Christ
To be our guide and thine."

"Go you down, go you down to yonder town
And sit in the gallery;
And there you'll find sweet Jesus Christ
Nailed to a big yew-tree."

So down they went to yonder town,
As far as foot could fall,
And many a grievous bitter tear
From the virgins' eyes did fall.

"O peace, mother, O peace, mother,
Your weeping doth me grieve;
O I must suffer this" he said,
"For Adam and for Eve."

"O how can I my weeping leave,
Or my sorrows undergo,
Whilst I do see my own Son die
When sons I have no mo?"

"Dear mother, dear mother, you must take John
All for to be your son,
And he will comfort you sometimes,
Mother, as I have done."

"O come thou John Evangelist,
Thou'rt welcome unto me,
But more welcome my own dear son
That I nursed upon my knee."

Then he laid his head on his right shoulder,
Seeing death it struck him nigh;
"The Holy Ghost be with your soul,
I die, mother dear, I die."

Oh, the rose, the rose, the gentle rose,
And the fennel that grows so green!
God give us grace in every place
To pray for our king and queen.

Furthermore for our enemies all
Our prayers they should be strong.
Amen! good Lord! your charity
Is the ending of my song.

This is a difficult ballad to understand, and its message is not easy to come by. The best light so far to have been shed on this poem comes from a very beautiful East Anglian illumination of the early fourteenth century known as the "Arundel Psalter". In this psalter two subjects are dealt with – "The Tree of Death" and "The Tree of Life". "The Tree of Death" is portrayed in dull colours, and its branches bear only a very few poorly developed leaves. The Serpent winds itself round the trunk of the tree, beside which Adam and Eve stand one on either side. For fruit, the tree bears seven labels each inscribed with one of the Seven Deadly Sins, and below them hang seven smaller discs representing the secondary sins that follow in consequence. Sullen creatures perch on the branches of the tree whose lean and tapering form signifies dissoluteness and corruption, while at the very top, perches a moth – the symbol of death. On another page and in the brightest of colours is depicted "The Tree of Life". The tree, whose trunk and branches are of gold, gives forth a mass of gleaming foliage whose leaves it is interesting to note, are those of the vine. From the golden boughs spring seven beautiful Virtues, each of which bears its own fruit or minor virtues. Within the shade of the branches and with a heavenly tranquillity, four beautiful ladies in the rôle of the Cardinal Virtues – pursue their way. At the foot of the tree stands the Blessed Virgin with the Archangel Gabriel in attendance. The trunk is a signpost pointing the way to Eternal Life, and at its summit is the Divine Face adored by two winged angels. We have then beneath "The Leaves of Life" the "Seven Virtues" and the Blessed Virgin; and under "The Leaves of Death" the two people for whom, as the ballad says, Christ was to suffer:

"O peace, mother, O peace, mother,
Your weeping doth me grieve;

O I must suffer this" he said,
"For Adam and for Eve."

The tree therefore signifies the cross upon which Christ died, while the vine-leaves are a metonymy signifying the fullness of the Christian Way of Life with its roots in the Redemption of Christ.[64]

Cecil Sharp points out that the words of a folk-ballad only begin to deteriorate when the singer has ceased to understand their meaning, and he quotes the two opening lines of "Little Sir Hugh" as they were sung by a very bright and intelligent singer:

Do rain, do rain, American corn,
Do rain both great and small.

By comparing these lines with other versions of the same song Sharp discovered that they were but a corruption of:

It do rain, it do rain in merry Lincoln,
It do rain both great and small.

Similarly, in the ballad "The Leaves of Life" the line in the fourth verse which runs: "And sit in the gallery", has been shown to be a corruption of: "To that citie in Galilee". The text had become unintelligible only after Christianity itself had become unintelligible for want of religious instruction.

In folk-language,[65] although "the red rose-bud" is generally used as a symbol of "wantonness", "the rose" and "the rose without a thorn" are terms that expressly refer to the Blessed Virgin. Like the "holly", the "fennel" (which can denote either parsley or laurel), signifies the righteous in general, and Christ in particular. It is likely also, that the expression "Leaves of Life" may have been partially inspired by the professional herbalist in an age of primitive medicine. Finally it is worth noting that, as the motets of the Fayrfax book clearly show, the Passion of Christ was the favourite theme among composers of the late fifteenth and early sixteenth centuries. It could well be that these devotional works that had their liturgical expression in the "Jesus-Mass" were but the artistic outcome of the same devotion that had sprung up among the English country-folk at a much earlier period, to which so many Franciscan crucifixion ballads including "The Leaves of Life" belong. Moreover, it is not inconceivable that the Thomas of the third verse might refer to St Thomas of Canterbury who gave his life in defence of the rights of the Church against Henry II (1133-1189), and the lamentations of the holy virgins an allusion to the anxiety felt among the religious women of the period so vividly described by T. S. Eliot. It is equally likely that the Westminster Sequence composed by a Londoner and found in the Great Missal presented to Westminster Abbey by Abbot Litlington (1362-1386) was the liturgical expression of current ballad sentiments:

Hi triumphant in agone,
Hi de Christi passione,
Sibi pingunt stigmata.

Jam exutus tunica
Thomas, ope medica
Florescit per secula.

However, in whatever way we decide to interpret this beautiful ballad, as Percy Dearmer remarks: "This is a fine example of the way in which a mystical vision is created by the best folk-poetry." Later broadside ballads lacked such beauty.

The ballad was printed on a "broadside" or "broadsheet", and although both these terms are in use today and employed indiscriminately, the correct name for any printed sheet of paper in which the matter is so arranged as to be read unfolded, is "broadside". The size of the sheet is of no consequence; a tradesman's handbill is just as much a broadside as the largest of ballad sheets. If the sheet is folded once it is a folio; folded twice it becomes a quarto folio, three times – an octavo folio and so on. Most broadsides printed only the text of the ballad and few broadsides with music have yet been discovered.

Many of the ballad sheets inscribe the names and the addresses of the printers, for instance: John Gough (1540), of Cheapside, "at the signe of the Mermayd"; John Redman (1540) of Paternoster Row, "at the signe of our Ladye"; Richard Jones (1584) of Fleet Street. Early ballad sheets were very large and the poems were printed across the long or broad side of the paper. In Shakespeare's day (cf. *The Winter's Tale*, Act IV, Sc. iv, 261-300), broadsides were distributed among the country-folk by pedlars, while the ballad singers and the stationers' stalls sold them as "stall copies" in the towns; and although carol singing had almost disappeared, even in the lifetime of Charles Dickens (1812-1870) the ballad vendor could still be seen on his rounds (cf. *The Seven Poor Travellers*, Chap. 1, 1854). Occasionally the broadside was pressed into political use and became an instrument of Party propaganda, and it was for this reason that Henry VIII forbade them to be printed. As a rule, the ballad was printed on one side of the paper only which enabled it to be pasted on cupboard doors and kitchen walls, and in the parlours of country ale-houses; and because it was continually being folded, and folded again, and carried about under the arm and in the pocket like a newspaper, it very quickly arrived at a stage of disintegration. This probably accounts for the rarity of fifteenth-century ballad sheets, for as yet we have no broadside dating earlier than 1535.

Throughout the whole of the seventeenth century, broadsides were printed in the same black lettering of the Gothic style as were the Bibles and legal documents of the period in order that they might appear more ancient than they really were. They were frequently adorned with crudely fashioned wood engravings which might include a musical quotation indicating the tune to which the ballad was to be sung, but many of these references still remain unidentified.

A "garland" was a broadside folded twice, and measured about seven and a half inches long by five inches wide, with the front page displaying a large woodcut. At one time a garland would include twenty or thirty pages of ballad literature, but by the eighteenth century it had reverted to its original form and remained in crown quarto folio till the middle of the nineteenth century. By 1800 the ballad sheet had become very like our modern galley proofs, and later still was issued in long sheets three feet in length, carrying four columns of type, and sold as "three yards of comic song a penny".

For many years London was the home of the broadside and the garland, and the main centres of ballad printing were St Paul's Churchyard, Cheapside, Paternoster Row, Holborn, Smithfield, and London Bridge. The ballads of William Dicey (1730) bore the imprint "printed and sold in Bow Church Yard", and "Johnny Pitts", who was known to operate from 14 Great St Andrew's Street, Seven Dials, was said to have been a bum-boat woman serving the Fleet with tobacco, knick-knacks, and ballad sheets. In 1813 James Catnach opened a press at 2 and 3 Monmouth Court, Seven Dials, but by this time printing works had arisen in most parts of the country, and song sheets with both words and music were available everywhere.[66]

Apart from being sung by the country-folk in ale-houses, by packmen and itinerant ballad singers, the ballad was very popular among the waits. The name "wait", from which the surname Wakeman is derived, was applied to the public official or watchman who patrolled the streets at night time to ensure the maintenance of law and order during the hours of sleep. He was also something of a fire-watcher in an age when timber was the chief element in almost all buildings. Like the watchman in *Die Meistersinger*, he carried a horn or hautboy which he used to sound the hours and to reassure the towns-folk that he was on the beat and that all was well. Its loud and coarse sounding tone was ideal for out-of-door use, especially in times of inclement weather. Eventually these musicians clubbed together to form small orchestras, and at Christmas time delighted the public with recitals of their music. Needless to say, this was only after the quality of the hautboy had been improved, and when playing for pleasure and to while away the lonely hours, could be safely indulged in without fear of causing annoyance to the public. The first waits seem to have appeared about the end of the fourteenth century, and early in the fifteenth century, we find in the *Liber Niger Domus Regis* in which an account was kept of Royal expenditure during the reign of Edward IV (1442-1483) the following entry:

> A wayte, nyghtely from Mychelmas to Shrove Thorsday pipe the watch within this court fowere tymes. In the Somere nyghtes three tymes and maketh bon gayte to every chamber doare and offyce, as well for feare of pyckerers and pilfers.

The very first band or consort of waits was formed at Exeter in the year 1400, and then began a tradition of popular and public music-making that only began to decline in 1815 with the introduction of "the peace preservation police" by Sir Robert Peel (1788-1850). The waits fulfilled a great variety of purposes: they were called upon to perform on civic occasions, and to welcome the weary traveller as the stage-coach pulled in at the Inn.[67] It was not unknown for the waits to come to the rescue of a young man during his courtship, and in a fashionable seventeenth-century newspaper it was recorded:

> There is scarcely any young man of fashion who does not make love with the town music. The waits often help him through his courtship, and my friend Banister has told me that he was proffered five hundred pounds by one fellow to play but one winter under the window of a lady.

The waits of London, Chester, and Norwich were the most famous – the last named particularly for their singing. Each band had its own signature tune, its own costume, and its own "waits badge" incorporating the arms of the borough to which it was attached. The waits of the City of London wore blue gowns with red sleeves, caps, and silver chains or necklaces – all of which were stamped with the arms of the City. Many of the Bach family were waits, and Orlando Gibbons (1583-

1625) was one of the waits of Cambridge. The luxury of continually being attended by the music of the waits was hard to give up, and in 1589 Sir Francis Drake obtained permission to take them with him on his voyage to Portugal!

Most of us at some time or other in our lives have experienced a thrill of joy and exhilaration upon hearing the waits or the carol singers during the nights of Advent. In his *Sketch Book*, the American novelist Washington Irving tells how, in the year 1820 while on a visit to Yorkshire, he was pleasantly surprised by a visit from the waits one wintry night:

> I had scarcely got into bed, when a strain of music seemed to break forth in the air just below the window. I listened, and found that it proceeded from a band which I concluded to be the waits from a neighbouring village. I listened with hushed delight; even the sound of the waits, rude as may be their mistrelsy, breaks upon the midnight watches of a winter night with the effect of perfect harmony.

The music in question would probably have been "Christians Awake" – the first song of Christmas Day. The text was written by John Byrom (1691-1763) at the request of his eleven-year-old daughter Dolly who had asked for a poem as her Christmas present. Strictly speaking it is not a ballad, but it was an item for which the waits seemed always to have a particular affection.

Chapter 3

Folk Poetry

In the course of an interview given in the Home Service of the B.B.C., Frank Sheed was asked what he thought being a Christian amounted to in ordinary every-day life. He said in reply, that being a Christian meant "seeing God in everything". He could not have epitomized life in mediaeval England more succinctly, for in the fifteenth century the Christian religion was something that influenced the whole of the working-man's day, and permeated everything he did. God entered just as much into the chores of the housewife and the agricultural life of the peasant as into the pious offices of the verger at Mass time on a Sunday morning. As the most loved and widely known of folk-carols "The Holly and the Ivy" clearly shows – the life of the mediaeval Englishman was essentially contemplative. He saw God in the chattering brook – in the song of the nightingale – in the hoot of an owl:

O the rising of the sun,
And the running of the deer,
The playing of the merry organ,
Sweet singing in the choir.

It was during the fifteenth century that English carol literature reached its peak. The carol arose not only as the result of Chaucerian and Humanistic influence, but as part of a movement that had begun as far back as the ninth century. With the rise of the art of troping we see the first signs of the emancipation of the common people from the old austerity and the "traditional conservatism of the Church which for so long had forbidden the dance and the drama, denounced communal singing and frowned on any tendency of the faithful to desport themselves on feast days".[68] For centuries the people had clamoured for something less severe than the old plainsong melodies, and in the twelfth century their dramatic spirit was in revolt.[69] Anthems, tropes, sequences were sung with increasing dramatic emphasis, until eventually, from the liturgical drama of the sanctuary the Mystery drama and the carol evolved. It was the age of the secularizing of the arts in which as we know, St Francis of Assisi was one of the first in the field.

The Mystery Play was a dramatization of a Bible story. The subject matter of the drama was often determined not only by the guild members themselves but by some special feature of the locality. For example, "The Marriage Feast of Cana" was invariably produced by the Guild of Vintners. At York "The Building of the Ark" was performed by the Guild of Shipwrights. At Chester it was the tradition for the Guild of Watermen to present "The Ark and the Flood". It is sometimes claimed that the Mystery drama dates back as far as the fourth century, but although it was found in France at an early date, its first appearance in England was at Dunstable in Bedfordshire in 1110. The performing of a Mystery Play was an occasion of tremendous enthusiasm. It was looked upon not only as an outward profession of Christian belief but also as the highest form of entertainment. Nowhere in the country was the drama more popular than at Chester, and on one occasion twenty-four performances were given in the course of a single day. It was for the Mystery drama that a great deal of folk poetry was originally intended, and much carol literature purposely composed.

At first these carols were intended, as were the organ concertos of Handel (1685-1759) as intermezzi or interludes to entertain the audience during the interval. Later, singers took the stage led by a musician carrying a portable organ strapped to his shoulders, blowing with his left hand and fingering with his right. The carollers would process to and fro across the stage to the great delight of the crowd. Enthusiasm would sometimes reach such a height that the procession would leave the stage and parade out into the street and round the town – proof if ever there was one of the suitability of the carol form to processional use! The carollers were very popular, and keen rivalry arose between actors and singers. At Chester on one memorable occasion the singers had been called to the footlights so repeatedly that their repertoire became exhausted. The aggrieved audience not only set about the hapless carollers but wrecked the stage and reduced the entire premises to a shambles. It should be remembered that although these carols seem not to include a burden, many such burdens were deliberately omitted by the copyist not only because they were so well known, but because they were of the nature of "responses" and therefore not part of the authentic text of the playwright.[70] We can easily visualize how the mediaeval Englishman would revel in the following acclamations, stamping his feet as he stood in the crowd or stalked along in procession:

O, O, O, O, O, O, O, O,
O Deus sine termino.

Tyrle tyrlo,
So merylye the shepperdes began to blowe

By the end of the fifteenth century the carol had found its place in the Mystery Play and was sung as part of the drama. One of the most popular Mysteries was the Coventry play called "The Pageant of the Shearmen and the Tailors" specially written for the feast of Corpus Christi instituted by Pope Urban IV in 1264. A number of fine specimens were written for this pageant: "The Coventry Carol", "The Song of the Angels", "The Lullaby of the Innocents", and "The Song of the Shepherds". The play is remarkable for its childlike simplicity. The shepherds straight from the fields enter the manger to pay their tribute to the Infant King. One shepherd makes an offering of his pipe:

I have nothing to present with thy child
But my pipe. (Hold, hold, take it in thy hand.)
Wherein much pleasure that I have found.
And now to honour thy glorious birth,
Thou shalt have it to make thee mirth.[71]

"The Song of the Shepherds", written to be sung as part of the play itself, is a typical example of the simplicity and artlessness of the mediaeval folk-carol:

As I rode out this enders night,
Of three jolly shepherds I saw a sight,
And all around their fold a star shon bright,
They sang terly terlow,
They sang terly terlow,
So merrily the shepherds their pipes can blow.[72]

These charming specimens from mediaeval Mystery drama are alike in displaying a devotion that is as sweet as it is unself-conscious, and one carol spoken by a shepherd in a Townley Play shows that the practice common among infants of the present day – of placing small gifts at the feet of the Divine Infant in the Manger, is not such a modern practice after all:

Hail darling dear! Full of Godhead!
I pray Thee be near when that I have need.
Hail! Sweet is Thy cheer my heart would bleed
To see Thee sit here in so poor a weed –
With no pennies. Hail! Put forth Thy dall –
I bring Thee but a ball.
Have and play Thee with all
And go to the tenys.[73]

Our English carols may very broadly be divided into three main categories. There are the carols like The Wassail Songs of the West Riding that are best suited for use out of doors – the purpose for which most carols were originally intended:

Good Master and Good Mistress,
While you're sitting by the fire,
Pray think of us poor children
Who are wandering in the mire.

There are some few that are more suitable for singing at home in the warmth and comfort of the yule fire. Lastly, there are those mediaeval poems to which rich and beautiful counterpoint has been added by highly skilled composers of the fifteenth century and of the present day. These are for performance in church by a well trained and competent male choir.

One of the most popular carols is "Welcum Yule". The feast of Christmas coincided with the time the Druids kept their winter festival, and so in spite of their associations, a great many pagan customs were incorporated into Christian usage. The carol dates back to the fifteenth century and is believed to have been a particular favourite with the saintly King Henry VI (1421-1471). A second version dating from 1430 can be found in the Bodleian Library among a collection of poems by the blind Augustinian chaplain John Audlay. Just how popular this carol is with the general public can be judged from the "encores" it receives at the annual carol concert given by Sir Malcolm Sargent in the Albert Hall.

A useful carol for singing in unison is "All in the Morning" No. 17 in *The Oxford Book of Carols* – the finest of all our carol manuals, even if as in No. 34 the wording of some of the translations may be open to criticism. The polyphonic "conductus" was frequently used on festive occasions as a substitute for the "Benedicamus Domino" of the Mass, and in the fifteenth century when the "conductus" began to lose popularity, the polyphonic carol was often used in its stead. The Christmas season was a time of special licence, and although restrictions were eventually imposed by the statutes of bishop Odo de Sully of Paris, a free choice of music as a substitute for the "Benedicamus Domino" was always allowed as the texts of many polyphonic carols prove.[74] The cantilena "Deo gratias persolvamus" ends with the chorus – "Benedicamus Domino, Deo gratias", and the "Agincourt Carol" comes to an end with a burden obviously meant for the whole congregation – "Deo gratias". The carol "All in the Morning" may well have been used for this same purpose, for the music is strikingly similar to the plainsong melody of the "Orbis factor" in the Liber Usualis.

Unlike so many of our carols which are in the Ionian Mode, this is written in the Key of A Minor – following the custom among French composers who have always insisted on a more subdued style of writing for sacred or religious texts. The melody is gentle and plaintive, presumably because it deals not only with the Birth of Christ but also with the Betrayal of Judas, the Crowning with Thorns, and the Crucifixion. Here we see the Franciscan missionary at work – presenting to the people in the simplest of language the story of our Redemption.

The "Sans Day Carol" is not only one of the finest that has ever emerged from the West Country, it is one of the most beautiful specimens of all time. It receives its title from having been discovered in the village of St Day in Cornwall where it was taken down from Thomas Beard whose forbears had sung it for generations. This is a truly remarkable carol, for in the short space of six lines it covers the theology of the Immaculate Conception, the Incarnation, and the Act of Redemption. The holly or "Christ's Thorn" has always been taken to signify "Man", just as the ivy has signified "Woman", while "The greenwood", as in Christ's own day – denotes the just man, and "the dry" – the reprobate.[75] The meaning of the carol is clear: Christ in His innocence was the Second Adam come to restore to Mankind the innocence it had lost.

The holly is a particularly dirty tree (as will have been abundantly clear to anyone who has had to gather holly for his Christmas decorations!) for the holly does not, like other trees shed its leaves in the autumn, but retains them year in and year out together with an ever increasing amount of dirt and dust which is scattered by the wind throughout the entire tree making it as the carol says – "as black as coal". At the same time, the wood of the holly is greatly valued for the rare quality of its whiteness, and so the tree with its crimson fruit is regarded as emblematic of the Blessed Virgin mourning the death of her Son. This carol is one of the loveliest in the whole of our repertory, it speaks its message simply and directly, and with a deep and unaffected concern for the sufferings of Mother and Son which is so characteristic of these early mediaeval masterpieces.

Of all our carols the most difficult to analyse and unravel is without question the fourteenth century carol based on the legend of the Holy Grail. It is known by various titles: in *The Oxford Book of Carols* it bears the title "All Bells of Paradise", and again earlier in the same anthology "Down in Yon Forest". It is a strange and mysterious carol full of mystical significance, and as such would appeal only to those as are fully initiated into the glories of English religious traditions which are at the very centre of our national heritage.

The history and development of this carol as we have it to-day is unique, and may be briefly summarized as follows: well over a century ago, a carol that had been taken down by a youth – a member of a group of Morris Dancers from north Staffordshire – was in the year 1862 sent by an anonymous donor to *Notes and Queries*, a periodical founded in 1849 by William Thoms.[76] In 1905 Frank Sidgwick discovered that it was a variant of a mediaeval carol published in Flügel's *Anglia* (volume 26) of 1903 from a version noted down by the London tradesman Richard Hill in a Commonplace Book dating from the late fourteenth century and now preserved in the library at Balliol College. Frank Sidgwick's discovery was subsequently communicated to *Notes and Queries* in which the two versions – the new and the antique were printed side by side separated by four centuries. The version contributed by the anonymous donor appears as No. 184 in *The Oxford Book of Carols*, and in

1908 a slightly different version was noted by Dr Vaughan Williams and Ivor Gatty from a Mr Hall of Castleton in Derbyshire which has since been recorded in the *Journal* of the English Folk-Song Society for 1910. It can be found as No. 61 in *The Oxford Book of Carols* where "flood" has been changed to "river", and "foot of the bed" has been discarded for "bed's foot" – yet another example of the unauthorized meddling that is the bane of every folk-song collector. Of this beautiful folk-carol Dr Greene has the following observation to make:

> The best evidence that a given carol is true folk-song is the discovery in oral tradition of a version recently current. The only manuscript carol for which evidence of this kind has come to light is the Corpus Christi carol.[77]

The earliest version of this beautiful carol is of course that given in the Richard Hill manuscript as printed by Dyboski in 1908 for the Early English Text Society which we give here, although as Sidgwick says – the carol bears no title, and the term "Corpus Christi Carol" is used merely as a means of identification:

BURDEN: Lully, lulley, lully, lulley,
The faucon hath born my make away.

STANZA: He bare him up, he bare him down,
He bare him into an orchard brown.
2 In that orchard there was a halle
That was hangèd with purpill and pall.
3 And in that halle there was a bede
It was hangèd with gold so rede.
4 And in that bede there lithe a knight,
His woundès bleding day and night.
5 By that bede side kneleth a may
And she wepeth both night and day.
6 And by that bede side there stondeth a stone,
Corpus Christi wreten there on.[78]

As Cecil Sharp has confirmed as a result of his extensive

journeyings among the Appalachian Mountains of North America – folk-carols are exceedingly rare among the peasantry of the New World. Nevertheless an intriguing version of this carol was discovered in the early twentieth century and brought to England by Miss Evelyn Wells in 1936 who had noted both text and melody from a certain Amos Curtis of Brasstown, North Carolina. Dr Vaughan Williams quickly saw the resemblance to the version that he and Ivor Gatty had encountered at Castleton in 1908:

> Down in yon forest there stands a hall,
> (The bells of Paradise I heard them ring,)
> Its covered all over with purple and pall,
> (And I love my Lord Jesus above any thing.)
>
> Under that bed there runs a river,
> (The bells of Paradise I heard them ring,)
> The one half runs water, the other half runs blood,
> (And I love the Lord Jesus above any thing.)

The American version takes its title – "Down in Yon Forest" from the first line of the opening stanza, and we give it here in its entirety and in the form in which it was originally discovered. It should be noted that the thorn bush is unknown in Northern Carolina and so "shrub-tree" would appear a justifiable substitute. Furthermore – in the oldest of our English carols "Lady" is the term invariably used to rhyme with "Baby", so it would seem that the substitution of "Mary" for "Our Lady" indicates a native preference[79]:

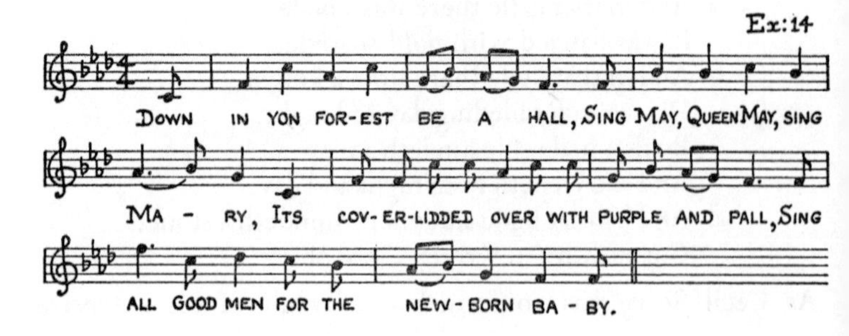
Ex:14
DOWN IN YON FOR-EST BE A HALL, SING MAY, QUEEN MAY, SING
MA - RY, ITS COV-ER-LIDDED OVER WITH PURPLE AND PALL, SING
ALL GOOD MEN FOR THE NEW-BORN BA - BY.

Oh in that hall is a pallet-bed,
Sing May, Queen May, sing Mary,
Hit's stained with blood like cardinal red,
Sing all good men for the new-born baby.

Oh at that pallet is a stone,
Sing May, Queen May, sing Mary,
On which the virgin did atone,
Sing all good men for the new-born baby.

Under that hall is a gushing flood,
Sing May, Queen May, sing Mary,
From Christ's own side hit's water and blood,
Sing all good men for the new-born baby.

Beside that bed a shrub-tree grows,
Sing May, Queen May, sing Mary,
Since he was born hit blooms and blows,
Sing all good men for the new-born baby.

On that bed a young Lord sleeps,
Sing May, Queen May, sing Mary,
His wounds are sick and see He weeps,
Sing all good men for the new-born baby.

Oh hail yon hall where none can sin,
Sing May, Queen May, sing Mary,
'Cause hit's gold outside and silver within,
Sing all good men for the new-born baby.

As has already been said, the significance of this carol in all its variants is of all our Christmas songs the most difficult to decipher, although there is a great deal of symbolism that is obvious in its implication. For instance, the burden of the fourteenth century version is a lament at the supplanting of the Gallican Epiklesis introduced about the time of Pope Gelasius I (492-496) by the "Supplices te rogamus" which was inserted into the Canon of the Mass following upon the liturgical reforms initiated by the Emperor Charlemagne (768-814) who established the Roman rite as the official liturgy of western Europe.[80] There would seem also to be some analogy between the Knights of the Round Table with King Arthur at the head, and the Twelve Apostles led by the troubadour Christ become Man to save mankind from the tyranny of the Evil One. In the story of Christ's Passion the term "bed" may have several meanings each denoting a point in the sacrificial act of Redemption. It might be taken to mean the cross itself upon which Christ was racked, and at the foot of which the faithful maidens remained to the bitter end, long after the apostles and disciples had fled in terror. It could signify the High Altar of an abbey or cathedral church which in mediaeval times – and indeed even today wherever a national monument dates from the same age of Christian faith – was enclosed on three sides by rich draperies whose colour alternated with the liturgical rank of the festival, and the entire brocade supported by four oak pillars standing a little apart from the four corners of the altar. Incidentally, in all Masses commemorating the Passion of Christ, red is the liturgical colour prescribed by the Sacred Congregation of Rites for vestments, veils, antependiums, and any form of drapery. Finally, when we call to mind that God is the author of all beauty and the well-spring of all artistry, it comes as a surprise to the author of these pages to find that "the halle hangèd with purpill and pall" containing "a bede hangèd with gold so rede" has never yet been associated with "the large dining-room furnished" where the very first Mass took place![81]

Students of the Coventry Mystery Plays are familiar with "The Pageant of the Shearmen and the Tailors" specially composed for the feast of Corpus Christi instituted by Pope Urban IV in 1264. The theology however that inspired the festival had been clearly defined many years earlier in 1215 at the IV Council of the Lateran, and fourteen years later in 1229 Pope Gregory IX prescribed the ringing of a bell specially preserved within the sacred precincts to engage the attention of the faithful before the Act of Consecration. The version submitted by the anonymous donor in 1862 has an important bearing on this festival and we give the opening stanza here:

Over yonder's a park which is newly begun:
All bells in Paradise I heard them a-ring,
Which is silver on the outside and gold within:
And I love sweet Jesus above all things.

The second and fourth line of this stanza occur regularly throughout the entire poem – and not without reason. England has long been the home of specialized art-forms: the training of the treble voice is one such, the Lady Chapel is another, the needle-like pinnacles that top the belfries of such monuments as Lichfield cathedral is yet another. Bell-ringing or campanology is one more department of sacred art in which to this day St Martin's Guild has no rival the world over. The mediaeval campanologist wrote his huntings and his dodgings, his snappings, bob-majors and his grandsire-bob-cators with as much devotion and skill as Byrd would have composed for the choristers of the Chapel Royal.[82] Bells therefore figured very prominently in the life of the mediaeval Englishman. They called him to church, and once there, again summoned his attention for the Act of Consecration and the Elevation that followed. With this in mind, the carol does not seem so insoluble after all:

And in that bed there lies a knight:
All bells in Paradise I heard them a-ring,
Whose wounds they do bleed by day and by night:
And I love sweet Jesus above all things.

What conclusions then are we to draw from our very brief study of this – one of the most beautiful carols in our English repertory, interwoven as it is with Arthurian legend, the Quest of the Holy Grail, the legend of the Glastonbury Thorn, and the story of the visit to our shores of St Joseph of Arimathaea with the Child Jesus? Miss Anne Gilchrist thinks that there is nothing at all to connect the fourteenth century "Corpus Christi" carol with the Abbey of Glastonbury except that Avalon is but another name for the monastery in question.

On the other hand G. R. S. Mead who has made a special study of this carol has the following to say on the subject:

> The three specimens of this delightful carol seem to be folk-variants of, presumably, a Troubadour original, based on Grail-Material. In the various cycles of the Grail-literature, there are to be found without much difficulty important Folk-Lore elements cropping out from the general Christian ground. In other words, in all forms of Grail-romance, there can be discovered, in the symbolism, a Pagan overlap, or even, perhaps, several Pagan overlappings.[83]

We feel that there is a solution that may possibly fit the facts although the general slant of our thesis may seem to the academician to over-simplify a highly complex problem that is now widely accepted as insoluble. Due entirely to the highly efficient system of Roman road-transport very early in the Christian era, Christianity arrived in Britain at a very early period. Archaeologists excavating near the south coast continue to unearth Roman villas each with a Christian chapel where Mass must have been celebrated at a very early date. Christian theology therefore was first in the field – at least when compared with those traditional legends with which we have just been concerned. Most stories whether mythical, legendary, or historical include a villain who is eventually brought to justice, and a hero or heroine who is finally vindicated and lives happily ever after. Every story-teller invisages his hero as the ideal character – good, virtuous, chaste – with all heaven well and truly on his side. It is not inconceivable therefore that the perpetrators of our traditional legends should have given point to their fabrications by attaching to them for the edification of their audience events that had been handed down for centuries as part of apostolic tradition, and were accepted as genuine historical fact and Gospel truth. We feel that this may possibly explain the seemingly inextricable entanglement of fact with fiction. If this was possible in the case of Wagner – and it would certainly appear so from his libretti, surely it would be even more possible five centuries ago when every Englishman professed the full Christian faith!

A carol very popular in the southern counties of England is "The Joys of Mary". This type of carol has something in common with the Latin sequence, in that it contains an abridged and concise account of the life story of a servant of God. In "The Joys of Mary" the poet catalogues as it were certain events in the life of Christ that were the occasion of special joy to His Mother. The events usually enumerated are those that are commemorated year after year in the liturgy of the Roman Catholic Church: the Nativity, the Annunciation, the Visitation, the visit of the Magi, the Presentation, the Finding in the Temple, the Resurrection, the Ascension, the coming of the Holy Spirit, the Assumption of the Blessed Virgin, and the coronation of the Virgin Mary in heaven. The version with which the public is most familiar is that to be found in the *Oxford Book of Carols*; but here only three joyful events are included while three stanzas describe Christ's healing of the sick, and one dwells on the agonizing death of the cross. The melody that accompanies the traditional version of this carol is the one given by Bramley and Stainer, although where it originated still remains unknown. Anne Gilchrist (1863-1954) however has discovered a variant sung to a scurrilous ballad about John Wesley, and another adapted to the nursery rhyme "The Three Little Kittens" to which by reason of its peculiarly endearing quality it was particularly suitable.[84]

The carol is found in many versions – the earliest exhibits prefer to refer to the Blessed Virgin as "Our Lady" instead of "Mary". It is noticeable that the broadside copies invariably give only "Seven Joys" for which a variety of different tunes are available. One was discovered by Anne Gilchrist to whom it was sung in May 1907 at Blackham in Sussex by a certain W. Wickham who had learnt it from some tinker children by the name of Wright in Ashdown Forest. A little earlier in the April of 1907 Cecil Sharp in the course of his travels in

Gloucestershire had come across a second version at Old Sodbury which was still a favourite with a certain Joseph Evans at the advanced age of eighty-three. Yet another was noted by Sharp from a Mrs Nicholas living at Camborne in Cornwall six years later on 12th May 1913.[85] Miss Lucy Broadwood has recorded two Berkshire versions of "The Nine Joys of Mary" discovered by Miss Arkwright MUS.D. – one sung to the tune of "The Banks of Sweet Dundee", the other to the "Chestnut" melody or "God Rest You Merry, Gentlemen" in the major key.[86] There is also a Somerset version enumerating "Ten Joys", and a very early fourteenth century variant reducing the number of "Joys" to five.

This carol in whatever form it may take, is an extremely old one, and goes back to pre-Reformation times when the Franciscan missionary apostolate was at its height. In "The Joys of Mary" we see once again the friar at work – endeavouring in the simplest of language to instruct the country-folk in the basic truths of their Christian religion. It is not surprising therefore to find in the desolate period that followed the dissolution of the monasteries and the Cromwellian persecution a growing ignorance and a subsequent apathy in fundamentals of Christian belief that had been an integral part of the life of every Englishman since the day when St Augustine first landed on the coast of Kent. As Lucy Broadwood herself discovered – the old folk-songs were still sung by the peasantry of the seventeenth century, but alas, the words had lost their meaning. So we find "The first good joy that Mary had" relapsed into "The first good joy of Mary Anne" – pathetic and unbelievable, but a fact.

Before bringing our discussion to a close, we would like to include an unusual version of this carol discovered by Alice E. Gillington in the course of her journeyings through Surrey, Sussex and Hampshire. She received it from a half-gypsy woman who sang it as she nursed her sleeping baby. Incidentally, it was her husband who had contributed the "In Dessexshire" song – a ballad that is among the rarest of English folk-songs.[87] Here then is "The Twelve Joys of Mary" in a version that as yet I have never met in any anthology of Christmas carols:

Ex:15
Stanza:
(1). The first good joy that Mar-y had it was the joy of one: It
was to see her own dear Son when He was born a Man; When
He was born a Man, good Lord, And bless-ings may it bring, Praise
Fa - ther Son and Hol - y Ghost, to Christ's E - ter - ni-
ty. (Burden:) O the ris - ing of the sun, The
lift - ing of the day, While list - ning to the
mer-its of gold, And sing-ing in heav'n al - way! Sing
Al - le - lu - i - ah, Sing Al - le - lu - u - ee, Sing
Al - le - lu, the heav'ns are true, Sweet blest Al - lu - u - ay.

The next good joy that Mary had it was the joy of two:
It was to see her own dear Son when He went to school.

The next good joy that Mary had it was the joy of three:
It was to see her own dear Son when He began to read.

The next good joy that Mary had it was the joy of four:
It was to see her own dear Son to read the Bible o'er.

The next good joy that Mary had it was the joy of five:
It was to see her own dear Son turn water into wine.

The next good joy that Mary had it was the joy of six:
It was to see her own dear Son to cure the leprosy.

The next good joy that Mary had it was the joy of seven:
It was to see her own dear Son making the blind to see.

The next good joy that Mary had it was the joy of eight:
It was to see her own dear Son when He carried the crucifix.

The next good joy that Mary had it was the joy of nine:
It was to see her own dear Son to from the dead arise. (*sic*)

The next good joy that Mary had it was the joy of ten:
It was to see her own dear Son to open the gates of hell.

The next good joy that Mary had it was the joy of eleven:
It was to see her own dear Son ascended into heaven.

The next good joy that Mary had it was the joy of twelve:
It was to see her own dear Son when the Holy Ghost was sent.

It is useful to bear in mind that such carols of the type quoted above are not to be classed among the cumulative variety which include specimens such as "The Twelve Days of Christmas". Far from serving as tests of memory they were purely numerical carols purposely arranged in the form of a mnemonic so that the verses could easily be learnt by heart – yet another example of sound psychology on the part of the Franciscan missionary!

We have said earlier that the English carol according to the definition laid down by Dr Greene is "a song on any subject, composed of uniform stanzas and provided with a burden". The burden is a completely independent verse alternating with the stanzas and sung as a chorus. It is the burden that makes and marks the carol. What then are we to say of that multitude of Christmas songs so dear to the heart of the music-loving public which do not bear the hallmark of the burden but which have been known as carols for so long? Such examples are so numerous that they could form an anthology on their own: "Adam Lay Ybounden", "The Truth from Above", "The Children's Song of the Nativity", "Remember O Thou Man", "On Christmas

Night all Christians Sing", "The Gallery Carol", "This New Christmas Carol", "In the bleak Mid-Winter", "While Shepherds Watched", "The Sussex Mummers' Carol", "Come all you worthy gentlemen", and that most beautiful of all Christmas songs – "I Sing of a Maiden". These lovely specimens may or may not be folk-songs, but they cannot by any stretch of the imagination be classed either as hymns or ballads; they cannot even be regarded as the English equivalent of the French noël, for the noël is a song devoted exclusively to the Nativity, whereas songs such as the "May Carol", "Spring Has Come", and "Pleasure It Is" may be sung almost at will. How then do we catalogue this vast collection of English songs if they do not qualify for any one of the above-mentioned categories? These are the *carolites*, and they contain some of the finest of our Christmas songs, and a poetry of such beauty as is rarely found among the works of men.

CAROLITE

(by G.K.C., 1874-1936)

The Christ-child lay on Mary's lap,
His hair was like a light.
(O weary, weary were the world,
But here is all aright.)

The Christ-child lay on Mary's breast,
His hair was like a star.
(O stern and cunning are the kings,
But here the true hearts are.)

The Christ-child lay on Mary's heart,
His hair was like a fire.
(O weary, weary is the world,
But here the world's desire.)

The Christ-child stood on Mary's knee,
His hair was like a crown,
And all the flowers looked up at Him,
And all the stars looked down.

CAROLITE

Come all ye faithful Christians
That dwell within this land
That pass your time in rioting
Remember you are but man.
Be watchful of your latter end
Be ready when you're called,
There's many a changes in this world
Some rises and some falls.

Remember Job the patient man
The wise man of the East,
He was brought down to poverty
His sorrows did increase.
He bore them all most patiently
And never did repine
And always trusted in the Lord
And soon got rich again.

Come all ye worthy Christians
That are so very poor
Remember how poor Lazarus
Stood at the rich man's door
A-begging for the crumbs of bread
That from his table fell
The Scriptures doth inform us
He now in Heaven do dwell.

Now poor we are contented
Nor riches do we crave
Riches is all vanity
On this side of the grave
Although there's many rolls in riches
Your glasses will run out;
No riches we brought in this world
Nore none we can take out.

Cf. *Journal*, No. 7, 1905, p. 115, where a tune is given as collected in 1904 by Annie Webb at Weobley, Herefordshire, where it was sung by Mrs Wheeler, a charwoman seventy years of age.

The idiom of peasant language is characterized by a reticence, a courtesy, and a delicacy of expression that on first acquaintance is breathtaking to one reared in the atmosphere of urban society. Prior to the Industrial Revolution the English countryman had at his command a conventional mode of speech or "lingua franca" which could whenever necessary be called into use to avoid offending the susceptibilities of those members of the assembled company unfamiliar with their traditional habits of thought – especially on the subject of the fertility theme.[88] Accordingly the lily was a symbol of chastity; the morning dew invariably signified virginity; the flowers of the countryside bedecked with the morning dew represented the unsullied virtue of maidenhood; the feast of Saint Valentine ushered in the mating season, while the gathering of the young flowers of early spring typified love-making and consequent fertility. We need not proceed any further in our efforts to elucidate what must be one of the most beautiful poems that has ever been written. Only artistry at its most sublime could have justified the portrayal of a subject at once so sweet and delicate in its intimacy. This flower of flowers – cool and fresh in the early morning dew was plucked by a heavenly visitant, its beauty remaining undisturbed:

I sing of a maiden
That is makeless;
King of all kings
To her son she ches.

He came all so still
Where his mother was
As dew in April
That falleth upon the grass.

He came all so still
To his mothers bowr
As dew in April
That falleth upon the flower.

He came all so still
Where his mother lay

As dew in April
That falleth upon the spray.

Mother and maiden
Was never none but she;
Well may such a lady
Godes mother be.[89]

We cannot leave the subject of carolites without some mention of that most charming specimen of folk-poetry – "The Apple Tree". Anyone who has visited the tiny church of St Dunstan at Bourne End-on-Thames and seen the fourteen oil paintings portraying the Passion of Christ, could not fail to have noticed that these portraits, the work of a local artist, represent the events as having taken place – not among the sands of Palestine, but in the green hill country of Buckinghamshire. Here we see a practical example of the way in which native preference can influence religious and sacred art. People generally are averse to change; and village people in particular are set in their ways and like to conceive the Gospel narrative in terms of their native heath. We have already seen how the Newcastle ballad "I Saw Three Ships" was the creation of the seafaring folk on the banks of the Tyne, and similarly "The Apple Tree" folk-poem was a product of a folk community from the Cider Country.

The orchard has always been a feature of the English countryside, and in mediaeval England in particular apple and cherry orchards were the commonest of sights; in fact as Gertrude Jekyll and Sydney Jones tell us in *Old English Household Life* (p. 111) – cherry brandy was as commonly drunk as cider and beer which had been the national beverage for centuries. We should not be surprised therefore to find, as in "The Cherry Tree" ballad, "apple tree" or "cherry tree" preferred to "palm tree" with which the peasantry would be unfamiliar, or to find "apples and cherries" coupled together as in the second stanza of the version brought back from the Appalachians by Cecil Sharp. The peasantry were merely expressing themselves in the terminology suggested by the small world of village life.

At the beginning of the fifteenth chapter of St John's Gospel Christ uses metaphorically the example of the vine to explain the supernatural nature of His mission: "I am the vine; you are the branches." This symbolism was ideal for the people of Palestine most of whom were vineyard labourers for whom wine was a staple commodity, but the English peasant would have been far more at home with the apple tree and the cherry tree and had Christ in fact been addressing an English audience He would most certainly have adapted His metaphor accordingly. This incidentally might help to elucidate further the ballad of "The Seven Virgins", and "The Tree of Life" pictured in the East Anglian illumination of the Arundel Psalter where the Christian virtues are represented in the shape of apples, while the leaves themselves are those of the vine! "The Apple Tree" folk-poem is therefore the English peasant giving the parable of the vine in his own words.

"The Apple Tree" was discovered by Joshua Smith in 1784 and although found in New Hampshire it is a genuine example of English folk-poetry. There is alas but only one verse to which so far no folk-tune has been assigned. The musical setting which the choir of King's College, Cambridge, included for the first time in their programme on the Eve of Christmas 1965 was supplied by the Hertfordshire composer Elizabeth Poston. This lovely melody is to be found in *The Children's Song Book* (p. 58) which she herself compiled. Here is another fine tune by the same composer, admirably wedded to the solitary text:

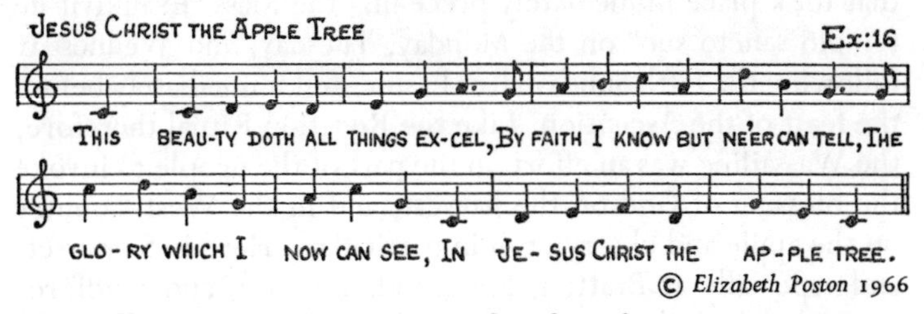
JESUS CHRIST THE APPLE TREE
Ex:16
THIS BEAU-TY DOTH ALL THINGS EX-CEL, BY FAITH I KNOW BUT NE'ER CAN TELL, THE
GLO-RY WHICH I NOW CAN SEE, IN JE-SUS CHRIST THE AP-PLE TREE.

The following setting by a Buckinghamshire composer was inspired and written at the village of Olney near the Chilterns. In the tranquillity of this hamlet the country-folk still preserve the religious beliefs of the fourteenth century, and it was from here that a contingent left for the New World in the late sixteenth century and established a settlement in New England which bears the name of Olney to this very day. It is interesting to note that the well-known "pancake race" that takes place in the Buckinghamshire village every Shrove Tuesday, is still preserved as an annual event in the American town of the same name. Here then is the tune from the Chilterns:

Ex:17
THIS BEAU-TY DOTH ALL THINGS EX-CEL, BY FAITH I KNOW BUT NE'ER CAN TELL, THIS
BEAU-TY DOTH ALL THINGS EX-CEL, BY FAITH I KNOW BUT NE'ER CAN TELL, THE
ritard.
GLO-RY WHICH I NOW CAN SEE IN JE-SUS CHRIST THE AP-PLE TREE.

The apple and cherry symbolism must have been exceedingly common in the heyday of English folk-song, and although genuine specimens are becoming increasingly difficult to come by, we still have with us examples of the apple and cherry imagery in the Wassail Songs of the Cider Country and Home Counties, the function of which was the secular equivalent of the liturgical Rogation Ceremonial – a series of processions that took place immediately preceding the Mass "Exaudivit de templo sancto suo" on the Monday, Tuesday, and Wednesday following the Fifth Sunday after Easter, and immediately before the feast of the Ascension. Like the Rogation Ritual therefore, the Wassailing was an effort on the part of the people to invoke the blessing of God on the harvest, and in the West Country on the apple and cherry crop in particular. Here in Somerset, and especially at Bratton, Stockland, Enmore, and Bradford-on-Tone, wassailing was restricted to 17th January the date deriving from ancient Saxon times for the keeping of the feast of the Epiphany. In *The Besom Maker* published in 1888 (p. 10)

Mr H. Sumner gives the following Wassail Song as sung by the peasantry of western Somersetshire:

STANZA: Wassail Wassail all round our town
Our cup is white and our ale is brown
Our bowl is made of a good ashen tree,
And here my kind fellow, we'll drink to thee.

BURDEN: Hats full, caps full, three bushel bags full,
(SPOKEN ONLY) Apple rooms, Barns and Bartons full.
Hurrah! Hurrah! Hurrah!

In the fifth series of his *Folk-Songs from Somerset* (1904-1909) Cecil Sharp gives a typical example of the wassailing of apple trees. Both the words and the tune employed in the ritual were taken down from William Crockford of Bratton, Minehead, who for years had acted as conjuror at the ceremony. As this type of Wassail Song seems nearer Druidic Folk-Lore than the Christian folk-carol we quote only the text (CXXVIII, pp. 72, 73):

THE APPLE TREE WASSAIL or SUSSEX "OWLING" SONG

STANZA: Old apple tree we'll wassail thee
And hoping thou wilt bear;
The Lord does know where we shall be
To be merry another year.
To blow well and to bear well,
And so merry let us be;
Let every man drink up his cup,
And health to the old apple tree.

BURDEN: Apples now, hatfulls, capfulls, three-bushel bagfulls, tallets ole fulls, barn's floor fulls, little heap under the stairs.

Hip, hip, hip, hooroo!
Hip, hip, hip, hooroo!
Hip, hip, hip, hooroo!

The ceremony took the following form: the villagers would meet in the orchard about seven or eight o'clock in the evening. Joining hands, they would dance in a ring around the apple tree as in the May Pole Dance – its Christian derivative. The stanza was sung during the dance at the end of which the burden was delivered with as much noise as possible – shouting, clapping, the stamping of feet, and the exploding of musketry. The stanza was obviously at one time a form of Druidic prayer intended for a precentor but which as with so much pagan ritual, passed into Christian usage. The singing and dancing having ended, a piece of toast soaked in cider would be placed on a branch of the tree as a protection against evil spirits. The company would then proceed to another treee where the ceremony would be repeated.

There is little doubt therefore that "The Apple Tree" discovered by Joshua Smith in New Hampshire is a genuine specimen of English folk-poetry. The story of the departure from the West Country of seventy-four men and twenty-eight women in the *Mayflower* in 1620 is a romantic and colourful one, and needs no retelling; but it was neither the first nor the last of such expeditions. Jamestown was founded by a colony of English settlers in 1607, and the Roman Catholic, Lord Baltimore established a colony at Maryland during the reign of Charles I (1600-1649). The puritan colonies established at Massachusetts and Plymouth Rock although militant in the extreme were insignificantly small, and the entire thirteen states stretching from Manchester and St Albans in New Hampshire in the north, taking in Smithfield and Oxford on the outskirts of the Appalachians, down to Saint Augustine and Lake Saint George in Florida, went to form the "New England" or "Greater Britain" where the settlers still clung to the religion of the Reformed Church of their Mother Country. The well known account of George Washington confronting his son who had chopped down his cherry tree would seem to indicate that this tree of his was one of his most cherished possessions!

"The Twelve Days of Christmas" is a cumulative folk-song for use at party games. It was originally intended as a song for "Twelfth Night" exclusively, but is now sung throughout the whole of the Christmas season. In London where it was extremely popular for over three quarters of a century, it became a game of forfeits or a parlour game, involving a considerable test of memory. Twelve players were allowed to take part, and each player, having contributed his gift was obliged to recapitulate all the gifts previously enumerated bringing the litany to an end with the words: "And a partridge in a pear tree," in which, as in a burden, the entire company joined. If a player failed to repeat the gifts in the correct order a forfeit was demanded of him. Lapses of memory were of course of frequent occurrence, and it is not difficult to imagine the fun that would be had in the playing of this game with all its humorous possibilities. It is not a carol, but it has always been one of the most popular songs at Christmas time.

The lady favoured with these innumerable gifts would need to have plenty of accommodation at home, for at the close of the festive season she would find herself the proud possessor of – twelve partridges in pear trees, twenty-two turtle doves, thirty French hens, thirty-six blackbirds, forty gold rings,[90] forty-two laying geese, forty-two swimming swans, forty milkmaids, thirty-six drummers, thirty pipers, twenty-two dancing ladies, twelve leaping lords – in all, three hundred and sixty-four gifts – one for each day in the year save one. Is there a gift missing? Yes – the greatest gift of all: the one to which these were but a prelude – the gift of himself.

As one would expect, the song is found in many different versions. It is such a rigmarole that departures from the authentic wording are almost inevitable, and so "a partridge in a pear tree" would become "part of a Juniper Tree" or "part of a June-Apple Tree", and occasionally "pass through a Junipear Tree", all of which variants were noted down by Cecil Sharp from folk-singers in Somerset. Unlike the versions to be found among the "folk" of the country districts, the text of the song as sung by the townsman is standardized; the manner of performance in rural areas is different too[91] and the singing of it in retrogression is unknown to the people of our large cities:

> Cumulative songs take a long while to sing, especially those that are retrogressive as well as

> progressive. The first verse deals with the first day, the second verse with the first two days, and so on, until the whole of the twelve days are introduced in the twelfth verse. At this point the verses decrease in length; the thirteenth verse dealing with eleven days, the fourteenth verse with ten days, and so on, until the singer triumphantly reaches the twenty-third and last verse, which completes the circle and lands him at the point from which he set out.[92]

In folk-lore the pear is an emblem of fertility and the partridge an emblem of the Evil One, while the pipe and drum – as in the Burgundian noël "Patapan" – because they combine so well together have always been regarded as symbolizing the harmonious relationship between the good Christian and his Creator. The presence of the Evil one in the genealogical tree would appear to be a reference to Man in his fallen state awaiting Redemption through the Passion of Christ.

The origin of the song is a matter for debate, but its refined and chivalrous tone, and the fact that it has always been such a favourite with the French, would lead one to suspect that its source lies among the songs of the troubadours of Languedoc which had had such a great influence on European music over the centuries. In fact it reminds us of a "chanson de geste" that has run to seed. The snatch of melody that accompanies the enumeration of the gifts, ending as it does with the Imperfect Cadence (IV-V) is almost identical with that used by the French minstrels of the twelfth and thirteenth centuries. Furthermore, why, one may ask, do the hens necessarily have to be French? – and what of the "dancing ladies" and the "leaping lords"? Are we back among the leotards and jacquelines of the dancing class? Is this an echo of "La grâce sautée" from French ballet? One wonders.

The first carol ever to appear in print in this country was "The Boar's Head Carol" which was published for the first time by Caxton's apprentice and successor Jan van Wynken of

Worth in the year 1521. It was composed as the result of an amusing incident said to have occurred in the early part of the fifteenth century. A man of learning happened to be walking from Oxford to the village of Horspath where he intended to hear Mass on Christmas morning. The road from Oxford to London runs over Shotover Common a derelict site on high ground. The scholar whose name was Copcot was engrossed in Aristotle at the time – when of a sudden, looking up, he saw a wild boar close upon him. He had little time for deliberation. Slapping the book to, he took the beast by the scruff and overpowered it by forcing the volume down its throat. He cut off the boar's head and carried it upon his staff to church where he left it in the porch. After Mass he took it back to College for dinner, in memory of which the carol is sung yearly at Christmas by the students of Queen's College, Oxford, to this day. The event is regarded as symbolizing the victory of the academic over the sensual, in token of which, it is commemorated in Horspath Parish Church by a window to the memory of the student. It is a carol of great antiquity and is found in many versions; it is always a boisterous carol as the following illustration will indicate, and is quite obviously only suitable for use at a Christmas banquet:

> Be gladde, Lordes, bothe more and lasse,
> For this hath ordeyned our stewarde
> To cheer you all this Christmasse,
> The Bores heed with mustarde.

Finally there are those masterpieces which are particularly suited for performance in church, and here we have some of the best music that has ever flowed from the pen of a composer: the *Ceremony of Carols* by Benjamin Britten. Not all of the items included in this work may be classified as carols; the Processional is a Latin text from the Roman liturgy set to a beautiful plainsong melody that is repeated for the Recession at the close of the ceremony. Both "Spring Carol", and "In Freezing Winter Night" by the Jesuit Robert Southwell (1561-1595) are carolites written in the style of a polyphonic motet – "Wolcum Yole" would have been an orthodox carol had not the composer dispensed with the burden altogether! Nevertheless, this contribution to our Christmas music is a work of genius for which we must all be eternally grateful. It is not merely a work of outstanding artistic value; it is a prayer, and no one can listen to this music without remarking to himself: "This man is obviously a devout Christian."

Edward Benjamin Britten was born at Lowestoft on the feast of St Cecilia in the year 1913. The youngest of four children, his father was a dental surgeon – his mother a keen singer. Benjamin began to compose when he was five years of age, and by the time he was fourteen he had already written ten piano sonatas, an oratorio, and a large quantity of songs. Prolonged study and hard work were the order of the day, and during his school holidays he studied harmony and counterpoint under his tutor Frank Bridge (1879-1941) a Sussex man from Brighton. In 1939 Britten went to America, but upon reading one day in *The Listener* an article on the East-Anglian poet George Crabbe, he fell desperately homesick for his native Suffolk, and returned to England in 1942. His *Ceremony of Carols* was written in the same year.

Benjamin Britten is at his best when composing for a text, and in his *Ceremony of Carols* there is that perfect marriage between words and music which distinguishes the great composer. The words he has chosen are among the finest examples of mediaeval poetry, and the music, scored for three trebles is yet another instance of how the fine arts blossom as the handmaid of the Christian religion. His setting of Robert Southwell's poem "This Little Babe" is superb: forward-looking and thrustful in its rhythm, it has all the energy and charming adventurousness that we associate with a small boy:

> This little Babe so few days old
> Is come to rifle Satan's fold.
> All Hell doth at His presence quake
> Though He himself for cold do shake.

It is pointless to attempt to compare one masterpiece with

another, but should we be permitted a preference then it must surely be the poem by an anonymous author in praise of the Rose of Jesse. When writing for the treble voice Britten has no rival, and in this carol – (although here again, Britten omits the burden) – where beautiful clashes of counterpoint gleam as nowhere else in sacred polyphony, we have what must surely be some of the purest music that has ever been written:

BURDEN: There is no rose of such virtue
As is the rose that bare Jesu.

STANZA: There is no rose of such virtue
As is the rose that bare Jesu,
Alleluia.

For in this rose containèd was
Heaven and earth in little space,
Res miranda.

By that rose we well may see
That He is God in Persons Three,
Pari forma.

The angels sung the shepherds to:
Gloria in excelsis Deo,
Gaudeamus.

Leave we all this worldly mirth,
And follow we this joyful birth,
Transeamus.

However, not all our polyphonic carols require the flawless technique of a cathedral choir, and there is one superb carol that presents no technical difficulties whatsoever to the most unpretentious of choirs that we feel we must not overlook. It is the late-mediaeval poem "The Virgin's Lullaby", by Richard Verstegan (1564-1620), set to polyphony of a later date and listed as No. 32 in the *Arundel Hymnal*. The music is arranged for three high voices and is so simple as to be well within the resources of any family gathering. Nanie Bridgman refers to the "Ave verum" of Josquin des Prez as "the Josquinian Miracle"; here then is "the little gem" among English polyphonic carols:

Stanza
Ex:18
(1). Up - on my lap my Sov-'reign sits, And feeds up - on my breast;
Up - on my lap my Sov-'reign sits, And feeds up - on my breast;
Up - on my lap my Sov-'reign sits, And feeds up - on my breast;
Mean-while, His love sus-tains my life And gives my bo-dy rest.
Mean-while, His love sus-tains my life And gives my bo-dy rest.
Mean-while, His love sus-tains my life And gives my bo-dy rest.
Burden
Sing lul-la-by, sing lul-la-lul-la-by, My lit-tle Boy; Sing lul-la-lul-la-by,
Sing lul-la-by, sing lul - la - by, My lit-tle Boy; Sing lul - la - by,
Sing lul-la-by, sing lul - la - by, My lit-tle Boy; Sing lul - la - by,
my li-fe's Joy! sing lul-la-lul-la-by, sing lul-la-lul-la-lul-la - by!
my li-fe's Joy! sing lul - la - by, sing lul - la - lul - la - by!
my li-fe's Joy! sing lul - la - by, sing lul-la-lul - la - by!

(2) When Thou hast taken Thy repast,
Repose my Babe on me;
So may Thy Mother and Thy Nurse,
Thy cradle also be.

(3) My Babe, my bliss, my child, my choice,
My fruit, my flower and bud,
My Jesus, and my only joy,
The sum of all my good.

(4) Three kings their treasure thither brought,
Of incense, myrrh and gold,
The heaven's treasure and their King
That here they might behold.

(5) And let the ensuing blessed race
Thou wilt succeeding raise,
Join all their praises unto mine
To multiply Thy praise.

The *Arundel Hymnal* is of particular interest to hymnologists and it is worth noting that it was the first hymnal to be issued for use by the Roman Catholic community of this country. The earliest edition bearing the "Imprimatur" (18th November 1901) of Cardinal Vaughan of Westminster appeared in 1902 under the following title:

> Arundel Hymnal & Other Spiritual Praises chosen and edited by Henry Duke of Norfolk and Charles T. Gatty, F.S.A. Published by the Editors from 3 Queen Street, Mayfair, London, 1902. Printed by Ballantyne Hanson and Company.

A beautiful frontispiece showing the Venerable Philip Howard imprisoned in the Tower (1587) introduces the volume, and the generous support and invaluable notes contributed by Reverend J. O'Connor are acknowledged in the Preface. The manual contains three hundred and eight hymns but no music, and is accompanied by a translation of a letter addressed to the

Duke by Pope Leo XIII (8th June 1898) which acknowledges "the first part of a Book of Sacred Hymns which you are engaged in publishing". The first edition of the *Westminster Hymnal* compiled by Sir Richard Terry appeared in 1912, and became the first hymnal to be approved by the Hierarchy for use among Roman Catholics. At this stage, the *Arundel Hymnal* now complete with music had been in use for some time; but Terry had other ideas, and during the tenure of Cardinal Bourne the "Westminster" manual – alas, to the accompaniment of much weeping and gnashing of teeth – gradually dispossessed its venerable, and certainly more elegant predecessor.

The hymnal of 1912 has fulfilled its purpose and now lies dead and buried; it will never raise its head again. The labours of the early pioneers from Arundel were not entirely in vain, and as with all things of sound artistic value much of their work such as the "Stabat Mater" by Croce has stood the test of time and is still with us today. The *Arundel Hymnal*, if only for the sake of one small masterpiece – "The Virgin's Lullaby" – was more than worth while.

In the course of this chapter we have touched on, and briefly tried to throw some light upon certain of our English folk-carols that are less frequently performed at Christmas concerts, and with which in consequence the general public are perhaps not so familiar. We thought we had completed our task and were preparing to bring the subject to an end, when in a flash, the astounding fact stared us in the face that we had overlooked the greatest folk-carol of all time, and the very first ever to be sung! We have to retrace our steps and go back in spirit over the centuries to the peace and quiet of the hill country of Judea to where the peasant folk were watching their sheep on the first Christmas Eve. It was here that the curtain went up on the first of the Mystery Plays:

> And there were in the same country shepherds watching and keeping the night-watches over their flock. And behold an angel of the Lord stood by them, and the brightness of God shone

round about them, and they feared with a great fear. And the angel said to them:

STANZA SPOKEN BY THE ARCHANGEL GABRIEL:

Fear not; for behold, I bring you good tidings of great joy that shall be to all the people. For this day is born to you a Saviour who is Christ the Lord, in the city of David. And this shall be a sign unto you: you shall find the infant wrapped in swaddling clothes and laid in a manger.

And suddenly there was with the angel a multitude of the heavenly army praising God and saying:

BURDEN SUNG BY THE ENTIRE CHOIR OF ANGELS:

Glory to God in the highest; and on earth peace to men of good will.[93]

Chapter 4

"Adeste Fideles"

In these days of liturgical enthusiasm, when the traditional spirituality of Holy Mother the Church is once more attracting men to herself as in bygone days, the "Adeste Fideles" is a call to Christian unity and an invitation to unite with one another as members of one great family in celebrating the anniversary of the greatest event in our family history – the birth of the Messiah.

It is no exaggeration to say that the "Adeste Fideles" is the most popular Christmas song in the whole of our English carol repertory. In the vernacular, it is in every sense a true carol, it has all the ingredients of a carol by which it is distinguished from the hymn, and it is unique in that it was inspired by the stanza-burden form of the Invitatory prayer from Matins of the Divine Office. It was born in the very heart of the liturgy, and in this sense may be called a liturgical carol – if there is such a thing. Although carol singing had become extinct by the end of the seventeenth century, yet strangely enough, it was precisely at a time of persecution while the Church was in hiding that England produced the carol that more than any other has endeared itself to the hearts of Christians the world over. Without being a folk-song it is an international possession.

Unfortunately most hymnals and carol manuals tell us little or nothing about the author of the "Adeste Fideles" and about the date of its composition. They are silent on the question. It is generally recognized, however, that it belongs to the eighteenth century and was composed within the lifetime of George Frederick Handel (1685-1759). Indeed any school-

child familiar with his little Gavotte in D or the Blacksmith Variations would immediately suspect the "Adeste Fideles" as having been the work of the great master himself so striking is the similarity of style; but happily we do not have to rely upon such mere conjecture as this. The melody of our carol was used to accompany the words of a satirical song sung in the course of a comic Opera entitled *Acajou* performed at "Le theatre de la foire Saint Germain" in Paris on 18th March 1744, and the text (of which Favert was the author) was directed to be sung to an "air Anglois" – an English tune.

Until recently there were six MS copies of the "Adeste Fideles" known to us and in each case the carol is found side by side with the "Domine salvum fac" and numerous other smaller items such as "Puer nobis nascitur" and "Tantum ergo". The music which is in simple triple time is written upon five leger lines and in the square notation of the plainsong. Each MS is signed and dated by the copyist himself and in a handwriting that is identically the same throughout bears the same inscription on the title page: "Ad usum chori Anglorum Johannes Franciscus Wade scripsit." Now Wade was not – as is sometimes said – a priest musician. He was a layman who made his living selling music, illuminating manuscripts, and teaching Latin and Church Music to the students of the English College at Douai. Moreover, like Jean Rousseau, another well-known copyist of his day, Wade would from time to time and as the need arose try his hand at composing in a small way. His name is found in the obituary list of the Catholic Directory of 1787: "1786 August 16th. Mr John Francis Wade a layman aged 75 with whose beautiful manuscript books our chapels as well as our private families abound, in writing which, and in teaching the Latin and Church Song he chiefly spent his time."

In 1946 a choir book of some two hundred pages of red and black musical notation and containing a very unusual version of the "Adeste Fideles" came into the possession of the Rev. Maurice Frost, vicar of Deddington, Oxford, who showed the MS to his friend Dom John Stéphan the historian at Buckfast Abbey, to whom he afterwards lent it for purposes of examination and study. The title page, alas, had been torn off, and with it the date and signature of the copyist, but the writing throughout the remainder of the book so closely resembled that of the other MSS as to lead one to believe that it had been penned by the same copyist. This is the Jacobite MS the discovery of which led ultimately to Dom John Stéphan revealing to us for the very first time in the history of music the author and the composer of "Adeste Fideles".[94]

The Jacobite MS so called because of the mention made of King James III in the "Domine salvum fac", is an expression of the loyalty of the English students at Douai for their king and country. Every week solemn High Mass was celebrated and sung by the students for the success of Prince Charles in the field, and the ultimate return of the Old Pretender to the throne of England. This is the only copy that includes the name of King James, and it would seem that the Jacobite MS was written at a time when there was still hope of the king's return to the throne – that is to say, before the unsuccessful rebellion led by Bonnie Prince Charlie in 1745. The Stonyhurst MS, it is interesting to observe, contains the name of King Joseph of Portugal who succeeded to the throne in 1750 the very year the MS was written. It would appear that the students at the English College at Lisbon for whom the copy was originally intended, transferred their allegiance to the land of their sojourn when it became apparent that there was no longer any hope of the return of King James.

Another unusual feature of this document concerns the chorus or burden of the carol. Where we are accustomed to sing "Venite adoremus" in the Optative Mood, the Jacobite MS has "Venite adorate" in the Imperative. Any cleric familiar with the Invitatory prayer at Matins would soon become aware of the offending lines, yet such a mistake would be only natural in a schoolmaster whose daily task was to ensure grammatical accuracy among the pupils of his Latin class. All this would seem to indicate that in this newly discovered MS we have one of the first editions – perhaps the very first edition – of the "Adeste Fideles" made before the writer had been notified of his mistake by someone more acquainted with the correct liturgical procedure.[95]

For all the above reasons, set forth at length in his masterly treatise of 1947, Dom John Stéphan is convinced that in the Jacobite MS written between 1740 and 1743 we have the first and original version of the "Adeste Fideles" and that both the words and the music of this lovely carol were composed by the modest and unassuming schoolmaster John Francis Wade, a copyist and teacher of Latin and Sacred Music to the students of the English College at Douai, where under his own personal direction it was sung for the first time.[96]

This in fact coincides with the opinion expressed by Arkwright in 1910 when he wrote: "My suggestion is that the 'Adeste Fideles' is nothing but an adaptation of a popular tune, eked out with reminiscences of a favourite Opera song by Handel. This adaptation by which a very fine tune was compounded out of rather incongruous materials may have been written by some choirmaster between 1740 and 1750 for the use of a Roman Catholic Choir."

During the Christmas season when the English carol fulfils its yearly commission of reducing us all – great and lowly – to the same common denominator as children of God and members of the same great human family, the "Adeste Fideles" will be heard throughout the length and breadth of the land: not only in our churches and cathedrals but in humbler settings, as when played by the waits in the market square, or by the poor man on his dilapidated instrument in a side street, or sung by the carol singers at our own front door. In whatever the circumstances, however, the message will be the same – a call to men to unite, and retiring awhile from the turmoil of modern life, to go back in spirit over the centuries to the peace and quiet of the hill country of Judea and to the place where God was homeless, and all men are at home.

Chapter 5

Mediaeval Piety, Its Return and Vindication

The great majority of our English carols were written in the course of the two hundred and fifty years between the death of Geoffrey Chaucer (1340-1400) and the expulsion of the Reverend Robert Herrick from his parish by Oliver Cromwell in 1647. Towards the end of the sixteenth century there took place in this country what has proved to be the greatest cataclysm in the history of the English people – the Reformation. It was the death-blow to all that the nation had ever held most dear. In all, seven hundred monasteries with all their priceless treasures were destroyed. Just how many polyphonic carols and ballad texts were lost in the wholesale destruction of broadsides and manuscripts will never be known. The Protestant historian Bale records that huge quantities of parchments – the accumulated wealth of centuries were used as waste-paper, and tells of how precious manuscripts were hurriedly despatched to bookbinders abroad "by the ship full".[97] If there was a lull during the Protectorate of Oliver Cromwell (1599-1658) it was because the destruction of the ancient culture was virtually complete, but for the puritan, Christmas still meant no more than "The Profane Man's Ranting Day" and "The Old Heathen's Feasting Day", and within twelve years the carol had all but disappeared from the land. Puritan doctrine may be summed up in the words of Hezekiah Woodward (1590-1675):

> We are persuaded that no one thing more hindereth the Gospel work all the year long, than doth the observation of that Idol Day once in a year, having so many days of cursed observation with it.[98]

In 1652 an Act was passed by the Government denouncing the celebration of Christmas and proclaiming the singing of songs in honour of the Blessed Virgin a legal offence,[99] and within a very short time carol singing became a thing of the past. Minstrelsy and ballad-singing were the next to go as William Chappell (1809-1888) points out in the preface to his *Old English Ditties* of 1861:

> Before the time of Cromwell every parish in town or country, if moderately populous, had its resident musicians, called waits, who were sometimes dignified by the name of minstrels. As there was scarcely a sport or festivity unaccompanied by music, these men found profitable employment. The evening dances on the village green were from Whitsuntide to Lammas Day. Harvest was then close at hand, and with harvest came rejoicings from farm to farm. Christmas furnished its indoor amusements and dances; Easter its holiday gambols. Now, on the contrary, owing to an absurd piece of over-legislation in George the Second's time, the innkeeper cannot have musicians to sing or play in his house without the trouble and expense of annual application for a licence.[100]

THE PURITAN

(by G. K. C., 1874-1936)

God rest you merry gentlemen,
Let nothing you dismay;
The Herald Angels cannot sing,

The cops arrest them on the wing,
And warn them of the docketing
Of anything they say.

God rest you merry gentlemen,
May nothing you dismay;
On your reposeful cities lie
Deep silence, broken only by
The motor horn's melodious cry,
The hooter's happy bray.

So, when the song of children ceased
And Herod was obeyed,
In his high hall Corinthian
With purple and with peacock fan,
Rested that merry gentleman;
And nothing him dismayed.

These verses were written as a result of a statement issued by the Chief Constable declaring carol singing illegal, and morally and physically injurious. He appealed to the public to discourage the practice. The earlier puritan was a merchant who inherited his capital from the confiscation of monastic property. Puritanism may be described as the regimentation of the country-folk in the service of big business, and mediaeval religion which had hitherto been so closely integrated with the chores of everyday life, was permitted only in so far as it did not interfere with the advance of mercantile prosperity. The puritan merchant was a lone wolf; the mediaeval peasant, happiest among his fellows at corporate worship, in the tavern, or on the village green, was first and foremost a community man with a community spirit. With the advent of puritanism, religion lost its element of joy. A man cannot at the same time serve both God and Mammon. The puritan preferred Mammon.

Fortunately, however, the printing of music had been long under way, and Wynkyn de Worde, who in 1495 had produced his first specimens of sheet music, had also as early as 1530 been able to place on the market a collection of songs with both text and music, and although a great wealth of carol literature must have perished in the destruction wrought by the Reformers, by means of the press some did survive in crudely printed broadsides as well as in chap-books and manuscript form. The folk-carol dragged out its precarious existence underground, while the manuscript carol came to an end altogether, and lay dormant, preserved in written record to await discovery at the hands of posterity.

The times were turbulent, and the outlook bleak, and all memories of the once "Merry England" were fast receding into the past like the magic-lantern pictures of a dream. With the accession of George I (1714-1727) and the establishing of the Hanoverian Dynasty in Britain, the image of England as "a land without music" soon began to take shape in the minds of German immigrants, and through the continual stream of visitors to and from these shores took firm root on the Continent where it remained for nearly two hundred years the common belief of Europeans. Charles Villiers Stanford writing on music in England during the eighteenth century does not mince matters:

> England, which had produced in Purcell one of the greatest figures in the time of storm and stress, relapsed into mediocrity. The few musicians she had were sound enough, but they shut themselves up in the churches, and did little else but produce anthems far inferior in inventive genius to their great predecessors. It is difficult to say if they would have produced another Purcell, but all chance of it was wrecked by the arrival of a great personality who had little respect for any of them, which he did not scruple to show, and whom we have to thank not only for immortal music of his own, but also for the decimation of the English School – George Frederic Handel (1685-1759). English music went into its shell: putting out its head

> occasionally to see how many foreign visitors were about, and not destined to emerge for more than a century and a half.[101]

Music therefore in every department was at a very low ebb. The fine arts have always flourished most as the handmaids of the Christian religion, and so it was that with the loss of the national religion the artist and his artistry were lost too, and the arts struggled on alone, independent of that vital inspiration the old faith had always quickened, and under which they had grown and flourished ever since the landing of St Augustine on the coast of Kent. Carol singing did actually revive a little about 1660 with the establishing of the first publishing firm by John Playford (1623-1693), but instead of the old songs returning, new ones were written of the "pork and pudding" sort that were scarcely more than eating songs. Sussex is well known for its folk-songs,[102] and from the heart of the South Country Hilaire Belloc writes:

> Songs are a possession, and all men who write good songs are benefactors. No people have so many songs as the English, yet no people sing less in these last sad days of ours.[103]

That visitors to these shores invariably find us "a sad people" cannot be attributed to climatic conditions alone.

About the middle of the eighteenth century there arose on the Continent a movement that later became known as the Romantic Movement, of which the key-note was the revolt of the personality against, as it was alleged – the tyranny of the intellect.[104] As a movement it had its points; and it was not long before the whole of Europe was caught up and swept along in the wave of enthusiasm that repudiated the false ideals of the Augustan age as represented by Pope and Boileau. In its beginnings it was essentially a literary and an artistic movement; in France it found expression in the drama of Diderot (1713-1784) and the novels of Rousseau (1712-1728), in Germany in the writings of Goethe (1749-1832) and Herder

(1744-1803), and in England in a renewed interest in Spenser, in Celtic mythology and "Northern Antiquities", and in particular in Danish and Icelandic literature as displayed by Percy (1729-1811) and Gray (1716-1771). The Romantic Movement stood above all else for a return to nature, and at least in the imagination – for a yearning after the joys of a simpler and a more primitive mode of life. This led inevitably to an aspiring after the ideals of a mediaeval past, to the reawakening of religious belief and the practice of devotion. There arose too, as may be seen in the pantheism of Wordsworth – a tendency to moralize nature and to relate the changing moods of creation to those in man, so that they became a reflection of his own joys and sorrows. Particularly noticeable was the influence felt in England among educated women. In philosophy the "Pietistic Movement" and the religious teaching of Gotthold Lessing (1729-1781) aimed at freeing philosophy from the technical difficulties that rendered it inaccessible to the general public, and so make closer contact with the man in the street. It was at this stage that Johann Herder the originator of the "folk-concept" was born, and we see here the first faint flush of what at a much later date was to appear as the dawn of a revival of interest in mediaeval English literature.

For a student of mediaeval literature to be unacquainted with Herder is as unaccountable as an English poet never to have heard of Chaucer. Who was Herder, and what kind of a man was he? Was he a mere rhapsodizing sentimentalist languishing for a dream-world, or was he a man of intellect who forwent the career of his choice to be able the better to adapt himself to the standards of the rank and file of his fellows? A short character-sketch recorded by Wolfgang Mensel about the year 1840 puts us in the picture:

> Herder was of a soft and yielding temperament; unimaginative and gifted with little penetration, but with a keen sense of the beautiful in others he opened to his fellow countrymen with unremitting diligence the literary treasures of

> foreign nations – ancient classical poetry hitherto unknown of the East, and rescued from obscurity the old popular poetry of Germany. In his *Ideas of a Philosophical History of Mankind* he attempted to display in rich and manifold variety the moral character of every nation and of every age; and while thus creating and improving the taste for poetry and history, he sought and revered God with childlike simplicity in all his works.[105]

Johann Gottfried Von Herder was a child of the Romantic Movement. Born at Mohrungen in East Prussia, he studied at Königsburg[106] where he attended the lectures of Kant and Hamann (1730-1788), and lived for a time at Strasburg in close friendship with Goethe. He was primarily a philosopher, theologian, and poet with no knowledge of music. Although influenced by the teaching of Hamann, he was far more affected by that of Jean Paul Richter (1763-1825) one of the very first romanticists whose *Dialogue on the Immortality of the Soul*, in the opinion of some, deserves greater recognition among Scholastics than it has hitherto received. It is however as a writer that he is best known, and his *Collection of Folk-Poetry* (1778) and *Ideas of a Philosophical History of Mankind* (1784) have attracted the attention of the ethnomusicologist ever since.

It was Herder who first created the concept of the "folk" and who, in his *Essay on Ossian* (1773) used the term "volkslied" – "folk-poetry" for the very first time. It cannot be emphasized too strongly that Herder was concerned with poetry, not with music. He drew a clear distinction between the "folk" and the "townsmen" – each as different from the other as the Indian from the negro. In the mind of Herder the "folk-concept" was an abstract idea of a natural and unlettered aristocracy of the countryside,[107] uncorrupted by ambition and the desire of "getting on in the world", and the expression of an inherent yearning for primitive simplicity and goodness, and a revulsion from scientific progress. The "folk" were the peasants – the "good", the "people" were the town-dwellers – the "bad".[108] The "unwritten literature" of the "folk" was "the living voice of the nations, even of mankind itself, to be heard under all conditions and in all places".[109] It was the language of a denomination common to all men; the common speech of humanity. To twentieth-century youth this might seem to be the concurrence of authority in the broadcasting of the barbaric noises so much to their taste at the present time, but, as though anticipating this Herder hastens to add: "It is no reproach to the noblest of poetry to say that it is heard on the lips of the common people; but by these people we do not mean the mob in the streets and alleys who never sing or make poetry, but only yell and destroy it."[110] All this makes interesting reading to the folk-song collector, for the carol texts that have found their way into broadsides or taken down from the mouths of the country-folk themselves are among the finest specimens in our English carol repertory.[111]

In the mid-eighteenth century antiquarian interest was stimulated both in England and in Europe by the discovery by Thomas Percy (1729-1811) later bishop of Dromore, of a Folio MS[112] containing a quantity of "vulgar poetry" written in seventeenth-century handwriting and the property of Humphrey Pitt of Shifnal. It has since proved a valuable contribution to ballad literature, and it was partly from this that Francis Child (1825-1896) published his *English and Scottish Popular Ballads* and Percy his *Reliques* of 1765 which did so much to awaken interest in mediaeval English literature. Excitement was earlier aroused among antiquaries at the publication in 1763 by James MacPherson of *Temora* or *The Lays of Ossian*, believed at the time to be translations from the original Gaelic[113]; it provided a great stimulus to Percy and Gray in their search for genuine specimens of ancient poetry, and in general created an interest in folk-poetry, and in the art supposed to exist among country-folk whereby they made their own peasant-poetry.

The "folk idea" has for a long time been the cause of a great deal of confused thinking among those who have been attracted by the countryman's way of life and habits of thought. The cause of the muddle is traceable to Herder's use of the word "volkslied", meaning "folk-poetry", yet so often wrongly translated as "folk-song". Moreover, the word "volk" is not found in many European languages, and the German term "volksmusik" used to describe "national music" or the music of the "folk" had no English equivalent for one hundred years after the death of Herder. The word "folk-song" is not to be found in any of the older Dictionaries, and it appears for the first time in the *Century Dictionary* of 1889. Carl Engel (1818-1882) musician, controversialist, and a universally recognized authority on musical instruments contributed in 1878 a series of articles to the *Musical Times* which was afterwards issued in book form under the title *The Literature of National Music*. Engel, himself of German extraction, would hardly have used the term "national song" as a make-shift translation of "volkslied" had the English word "folk-song" been in existence. By "national song" Engel clearly meant "folk-song" – not "folk-poetry" designated by the German "volkslied":

> The great majority of airs printed in Ritson's *English Songs* can evidently not be regarded as national airs in the strict sense of the term, although the tunes may have been for some time in popular favour. The same remark applies to the airs in almost all the English collections of old songs. The difference between a national song (volkslied) and a merely popular song (volksthümliches lied) is not always distinctly observed by the English musicians, and the two terms are often used indiscriminately.[114]

In 1866, fourteen years previous to the publication of the above mentioned work, Carl Engel published his *Introduction to the Study of National Music*. On the very first page he defines the term "national music" as "the music of a nation or tribe whose individual emotions and passions it expresses". He then adds in a footnote:

> The Germans call it "volksmusik", a designation which is very appropriate, and which I should have rendered "folk-music" had this word been admissible.

The term "folk-music" was certainly not admissible because it simply didn't exist and could not be found in any English Dictionary. Accordingly, "national music" (volksmusik) was made to include "Rule Britannia", the songs of Charles Dibdin and every kind of popular ditty. Moreover, of the thirteen hundred songs composed by Dibdin at the request of the Admiralty, exceedingly few have been found to survive among the folk. The peasant is a man of good taste, and given time is as good a musical critic as the trained musician.

Till now, we have concerned ourselves in the main with the "unwritten literature" of country-folk, with the view to showing how growing interest in ancient literature paved the way for a revival of interest in mediaeval poetry and ultimately to the revival of mediaeval piety as reflected in the carol. Before we proceed further, we should take a brief look at the interest shown in the philosophy of the "folk" by some of Herder's most ardent apostles, notably the two brothers from Hanau – Jacob Ludwig Karl Grimm (1785-1863) who in 1812 published his *Folk-Tales* and in 1835 his *German Mythology*, and Wilhelm, the author of *German Heroic Sagas* issued in 1839.[115] These two philologists between them did more than anyone to stimulate interest in the concept of the "folk" and to make the treasures of German folk-tale available to the world. By far the most loved of all these legends is that of Hansel and Gretel, since set to music by the most famous of Wagner's pupils – Engelbert Humperdinck (1854-1921), and performed for the first time as Grand Opera at Weimar in 1893. This beautiful work, now a regular feature of our English Christmas and cherished by children and adults alike, is frequently regarded as Everyman's introduction to Grand Opera. Richard Wagner (1813-1883) who like most children in his day and since was brought up on *Grimm's Fairy Tales*, explored Herder's idea of the "folk" to the full. He collected German folk-tales from far and wide and used them as a basis for his librettos which he always wrote himself. However, Wagner was concerned with the "folk idea" rather than with folk-poetry or folk-song, and while the term "volkslied" had come into existence long before he was born, the English expression "folk-song" translating the German "volksmusik" came into use only after his death.

Before we proceed to a study of "volksmusik" – and we should remember that the finest of our Christmas songs are folk-specimens – it would be interesting to consider the practical contribution the countryman has made to society through the "folk-product", particularly through folk-poetry and folk-tale. His contribution has been very marked indeed, as was quickly perceived not only by the early Gregorian composers, but by Charlemagne (768-814) in his efforts to unite the unruly peoples of his Empire, by the Franciscan missionaries of the thirteenth century, and not least by the apostles of the liturgy in their endeavours to spread the Christian message in our own day! The language of the "folk" is a ready-made means of gaining close contact with the multitudes as the Communist States have not been slow to appreciate.[116] The Greeks of old were very familiar with the Books of the Old Testament, particularly the Psalms and the "Canticle of Canticles", and a very great deal of a prophetic content must have permeated into Greek mythology and legend. Many of the Messianic prophecies of King David found expression in some form or other in the utterances of the Sibyls, and the similarity of the ideals enshrined in the "Song of Songs" and the legend of "The Phoenix and the Turtle" is far too strongly marked to exclude the probability of interdependence. In many ways the concept of the "folk" seems to be concentric with the doctrine of the Mystical Body of Christ, for even among seemingly pagan communities folk-tale and folk-poetry carry the seed of the Christian message in the rôle of a stowaway. How eminently practical then, was the psychology of the friars! Hansel and Gretel, who by hurling the Crust Witch to the flames free their fellow mortals from the spell of the Evil One and bring them back to life, is too forceful a reminder of the triumph of the second Adam and Eve to be allowed to pass without comment. The dominant theme of the *Flying Dutchman* – and Wagner was very far from being a Christian – that man's searching after freedom is to have its consummation only through the love of a pure woman, recalls at once the doctrine of the Incarnation; and in *Tannhäuser* where the redemption of the sinful meister-singer is accomplished through the holiness of a man and woman – the Virgin Mary is actually mentioned by name! In such wise therefore is the seed of Christianity carried by the folk's unwritten literature on the wind of fortune to lodge itself like thistle-down in some corner or crevice of a weather-stain, there to germinate and to grow in the hearts of un-tutored peoples. Again and again it has come home to the anti-quary that the folk-product has that mysterious potentiality for preserving what has been missed and lost by the literary masterpiece.

We now come to deal with the "volksmusik" – the music of the folk. As Dr Greene says – "folk-music is rapidly closing its accounts" and the specimens that we have survive from the Middle Ages onwards – possibly earlier. The first steps to-wards a revival of "national music" in the strict sense seem to have been taken somewhere in the middle of the reign of George III (1760-1820). Strangely enough, it was a foreigner, a young man named Jean Baptiste Malchair (1730-1812) who was among the very first to interest himself in English music and to try to find it.[117] He was born in Cologne and was the son of a watchmaker. Although a good violinist he had come to England to earn his living as an art master, but being as com-petent a musician as he was painter of landscapes he decided to make music a serious occupation, and in 1760 he accepted a position as leader of the Oxford Music Room Band. However, he always returned to his canvas with a will whenever time and opportunity allowed, and as he sat at his easel in the heart of the countryside of the South-Midlands backed by a small congregation of interested spectators, he would make friends with them, and jot down in his notebook which he always kept ready to hand, tunes that he heard them whistle or sing and would later compare them with those recorded in *The English Dancing Master* published in 1651 by John Playford (1623-1693). He communicated his discoveries to William Crotch (1775-1847) composer and organist since the age of fifteen at Christ Church with whom he formed a close friendship, and who subsequently published about thirty of his discoveries in his *Specimens of National Music* issued in 1808, in the preface to which he acknowledges on almost every page his gratitude to "Mr Malchair of Oxford who has made National Music his study". This was a good beginning, but it was early days yet and the Englishman's habit of self-depreciation as Cecil Sharp points out, was a continual source of discouragement:

> The Englishman's habit of self-depreciation has often occasioned remark. It is one of those national traits that is exceedingly difficult to account for. For centuries we have rested under the stigma of being an unmusical race, and so far from resenting the imputation, we have modestly acquiesced. So long as it was believed that we alone of all the nations of Europe possessed no folk-music of our own, it was, perhaps, a little difficult to do aught else. Even when at last the folk-song collector has laid bare the facts and exposed the hollowness of the ancient superstition, the old prejudice still persists. A few enthusiasts have become converts, but the majority still slumber on in the old misbelief.[118]

The interest aroused by Malchair and Crotch in the national folk-music of England eventually awakened a kindred interest among antiquaries and musicians in the religious folk-carols of the pre-Reformation period, and the first steps towards a revival of the mediaeval carol were taken about the year 1790 when Harward of Tewkesbury published his *Choice Collections of Songs* which included the texts of two folk-songs – "On Christmas Night all Christians Sing", and "A Virgin Most Pure". Progress was still very slow at this stage, and when Charles Dickens (1812-1870) wrote his *Christmas Carol*, although the waits were still heard, carol singing was almost extinct. About the same time, William Hone (1780-1842) published his *Every Day Book* where he gives an account of May-Day folk-lore and the words of "The Cherry Tree Carol" taken from a Coventry Mystery Play; but he did not hold out much hope for carol singing in the future. Then in 1820 William Litton Viner, a West-Country organist and composer, produced a collection of *Nine Christmas Carols* most of which seem to have been written in and around Penzance, and included "Come Saints and Sinners", "Thus Gabriel Sang", and "Bright and Joyful was the Morn". Two years later in 1822 came the first major contribution when Davies Gilbert[119] (1767-1839) published his *Ancient Christmas Carols*; there were eight songs in all for two and three voices which were augmented in the following year by twelve more, but only one new tune appeared. It is here that we meet "A Virgin Unspotted" set to the very beautiful tune with the flattened seventh, and the three folk-songs – "The Sinner's Redemption", "Joseph and Mary", and "The Lord at first did Adam Make". An interesting version of "The First Nowell" with a feminine star in the fourth verse is also included:

> And at Bethlehem Jury she took up her rest
> And there she did both stop and stay
> Right over the house where the King did lay.

Sustained by so little encouragement and the slender hope of their researches being valued by posterity, we cannot but admire the perseverance of these early collectors who combined to give us our first modern collection of Christmas folk-songs. In his preface, Gilbert tells us how it was that he came to undertake the work: "The Editor is desirous of presenting the carols in their actual forms, however distorted by false grammar or by obscurities, as specimens of times now passed away and of religious feelings superseded by others of a different cast. He is anxious also to preserve them on account of the delight they afforded him in his childhood."

In 1833 William Sandys[120] (1792-1874) published his *Christmas Carols Ancient and Modern* at the same time deploring the fact that carol singing was becoming more neglected with every year that passed. This selection gives the texts of thirty-four Christmas songs – none of which have so far been noted from oral communication; on the other hand, most of the songs gathered from the West Country that make up the second chapter have since been taken down from the country-folk themselves and are therefore classified as folk-songs. Sandys' collection[121] is the only one to give both the text and the tune of the Passion-tide carol "My Dancing Day". In 1831 John William Parker, a London printer whose business was bought by Longmans in 1863, brought out his *Christmas Carols or Sacred Songs* with a musical accompaniment, but with the exception of one carol tune they amount to little else than an assortment of hymns of a poor quality. Nevertheless, the venture was not entirely in vain, and the edition had an unforeseen value. In the preface, which contains an extract from a Latin poem entitled "The Popish Kingdom or the Reign of Antichrist" by Thomas Naogeorgus, and translated in 1570 by Barnabe Googe (1504-1594), there is unmistakable evidence of a revival of interest in the feast of Christmas, in Christmas customs and in carol singing:

> Then comes the day wherein the Lord did bring his berth to pass
> Whereas at midnight up they rose and every man to Masse.
> Three Masses every priest doth sing upon that solemn day
> With offerings unto every one and so the more may play.
> This done a woodden childe in clowtes is on the aulter set
> About the which both boyes and gyrles do daunce and trymly jet

> And Carrols sing in prayse of Christ and for to helpe them heare
> The organs aunswere every verse with sweet and solemn cheare.
> The priests do rore aloud and round about their parents stand
> To see the sport and with their voyce do help them and their hand.

Between 1836 and 1856 Thomas Wright (1810-1877) began to publish carols from the Sloan MS (2593) providing the music for a number of Sandys' poems to which no tune had hitherto been assigned, and so there emerged the first manual of Christmas songs for use in church. The foundations had been well and truly laid for a revival of national music.

The year 1843 is as familiar to the student of folk-song as is 1066 to the historian. It is a landmark in the history of folk-song, for it was in that year that the procedure of taking down words and music "from the mouth of the people"[122] was first followed by collectors as a scientific method. As to how it began, Margaret Dean-Smith has left us an account and we can do no better than give her own words:

> The Reverend John Broadwood observed that his parishioners in what was then a rural countryside – sang at harvest suppers, and wassailed at Christmas, and designating this "the silly sooth of spinners in the sun" set out to place these songs on record. In a commemorative article "A Centenary" in the Journal of 1943, Frank Howes has described how John Broadwood's retentive ear learned the tunes he heard, and how he played them to his organist so that they might be set on paper; how the arranger disputed the intervals particularly the flattened seventh ugly and barbarous to his ear (as it had been to Chappell's) but how John Broadwood persisted – blowing on his flute with more than

> customary vigour until each tune was written down as it had been sung. The little collection of eighteen songs and carols published in 1843, unassuming as it appeared was nevertheless a landmark – the first collection to be made of "folk-songs noted from the mouths of the people".[123]

In all but three of the sixteen songs where only one verse is given, the texts of the poems are given in full, and they are of particular interest in that they show the connection between the "wassail song" and the "luck visit" – a ceremonial visit to the people of the neighbourhood at Christmas time to wish them every blessing for the festive season and throughout the coming year, for which the wassailers received various forms of hospitality in return. It also shows that carol singing was still the practice in the mid-nineteenth century not so very far from London. This little collection which was issued a second time in 1890 under the title of *Sussex Songs* was edited by Lucy Broadwood and arranged by Birch-Reynardson, and bears the following inscription:

> Old English Songs as now sung by the peasantry of the weald of Surrey and Sussex, and collected by one who has learnt them by hearing them sung every Christmas from early childhood by The Country People who go about to the Neighbouring Houses singing or "Wassailing" as it is called, at that season. The airs are set to music exactly as they are now sung, to rescue them from oblivion, and to afford a specimen of genuine Old English Melody; and The Words are given in their original Rough State, with an occasional slight alteration to render the sense intelligible.[124]

It was a long time before these same scientific methods were used again, and when his niece Lucy Broadwood, whom Dr

Vaughan Williams regarded as "the greatest scholar folk-song is likely to know", began to tread in her uncle's footsteps, her contemporaries and even some of the founder members of the Folk-Song Society chose to remain aloof. John Broadwood was, in the words of Frank Howes, "a pioneer of the scientific method applied editorially to the oral tradition of English Folk-Song". Nevertheless, a great step forward had been taken towards a revival of English national music.

In 1846 *A Little Book of Carols* containing five poems with the tunes to which they were to be sung was published by Edward Francis Rimbault (1816-1876), organist and founder of the "Musical Antiquarian Society". Among the five were two folk-carols – "God Rest You Merry, Gentlemen" with a choice of tune, and "The Boar's Head Carol", and the Tyneside folk-song – "I Saw Three Ships".[125] Although Rimbault claims that his songs were handed down by oral tradition, all his specimens except the last-named were included in earlier publications, and it would therefore seem that he was the "editor" rather than the "collector" of the songs he enumerates.

In 1847 there appeared on the market *A Good Christmas Box* published by an anonymous collector of folk-song at Dudley in Worcestershire. It is a roughly printed chap-book lavishly ornamented with woodcuts, and contains some interesting texts that have so far never been published. There are two folk-songs – "The Twelve Apostles" and the Hertfordshire ballad "Under the Leaves of Life", a carol "The Saviour's Work" but with the burden omitted, and sixteen verses of the very beautiful Hertfordshire carolite – "The Truth from Above". It also includes the folk-ballad "Dives and Lazarus" and nine inelegant verses of the carolite "God's dear Son". Unfortunately some of the texts are of poor quality and it would appear that the editor included in the published edition lines of his own composing; but the quality of the verses was restored in later years after Dr Vaughan Williams had noted them down from the country-folk themselves.

It was almost fifteen years before any further addition to our repertory of Christmas songs appeared on the market. This was *A Garland of Christmas Carols* published in 1861 by an anonymous collector whose identity has never been satisfactorily established, and who is still referred to under the pseudonym of "Joshua Silvester". The collection was advertised as offering the public a selection of Christmas songs that had hitherto escaped the notice of collectors, and it gives a number of verses from seventeenth-century broadsides, printed in the neighbourhood of Birmingham and Worcester, that have since become well-known to the general public. The main item of interest is the folk-carol "The Holly and the Ivy" which was first printed on a broadside in 1710. "The Bellman's Song" is also included – a well known carolite that was sung by townsfolk on a "luck-visit"; a copy of the song with the good wishes of the Town Crier inscribed below would be pushed under the front door by the visitors who would later return to collect a Christmas offering for the bellman or night watchman – it was the urban equivalent of the country "Wassail Song".

In 1863 Rimbault published his second collection of songs under the title of *Old Christmas Carols* – a collection that has often been attributed to William Chappell (1809-1888) although there is no evidence to suggest that he ever published such a work. There are thirty-three exhibits in all, some of which appear for the first time with a suitable tune while others have melodies as given by Sandys, but restored to their original beauty. The following items are found prefaced by the reminder that carolling is on the increase: "The Angel Gabriel from God" – a folk-carol, nine unusual verses of "I Saw Three Ships" – a folk-song from the ballad country, "While Shepherds Watched" – a carolite with a melody in the major often used for "God Rest You Merry, Gentlemen", – "The Holy Well" – a folk-song from Derbyshire, "As Joseph was a-walking" from Somerset, and "All you that in this House be here" from Wiltshire. Unfortunately however Rimbault's integrity in the field of scholarship is open to question, and Miss Dean-Smith has commented firmly: "It is a pity that history has shown that Rimbault had few editorial scruples."[126]

In 1868 William Henry Husk (1814-1887) published his *Songs of the Nativity*; it was the first of the large editions that were to appear from then onwards. In all, there are about eighty Christmas songs collected from manuscripts, printed editions, and particularly from the broadsides of Silvester, but for whom many carols and ballads might have been lost for ever. The well-known folk-carol the "Holly and the Ivy" makes a further appearance except that – "now are both well grown" is given as a variant in the second line. He includes the ballad "Dives and Lazarus" too, but is of the erroneous opinion that it was not published till after 1860; in point of fact, it can be found in *A Good Christmas Box* of 1847. There is however in his preface the encouraging news that carol singing and the keeping of old English customs have been steadily growing more popular ever since the time of Sandys. Husk includes in his collection – a new version of "A Virgin most Pure" under the title "Come Rejoice all Good Christians", "The Bellman's Song" – a carolite with ten verses instead of the usual six, the folk-carol "Joys Seven" with a text from a Tyneside copy commemorating twelve joys, the text of "The Sinner's Redemption" and the folk-carol "Here we come a-wassailing", and a tune for "The Cherry Tree" ballad.

In 1871 there issued from the press, a work that had a unique influence on carol singing for over half a century. This was *Christmas Carols New and Old* published by the Rev. Henry Bramley, Fellow of Magdalen College, Oxford, and John Stainer the College organist. The editors claim, somewhat in the fashion of the period, that their collection has some newly-discovered specimens to offer that will be of additional interest to the public. Perhaps the editors refer to the Yorkshire melody of the "Wassail Song", the new Devonshire tune to accompany the folk-carol "The Angel Gabriel", and the music of "The Bellman's Song"; but however this may be, the two editors were men of influence and initiative who saw to it that their manual was put to immediate and practical use, and in this way a very great deal was done to interest the public in the singing of their national songs and towards a revival of carol singing throughout the land, as Percy Dearmer points out in the preface to the *Oxford Book of Carols*:

> The influence of this book was enormous; it placed in the hands of the clergy a really practical tool which is still in use after nearly sixty years. The great service done by this famous collection was that it brought thirteen traditional carols with their proper music into general use at once.[127]

Between the years 1876 and 1881 the "Sussex Mummers' Carol" was sung by the Christmas Mummers just outside Horsham, and was taken down by Lucy Broadwood[128] (d.1929) who recorded it in the *Folk-Song Journal*, No. 7, of 1905.[129] There also appeared in the same Journal the Hereford carolite "Come all you faithful Christians", "Lazarus", and the carolite from Sussex "On Christmas Night all Christians Sing". This was the beginning of a serious study of carol literature, and it was about this time that Miss Broadwood published her *Christmas Carols for Children*, and her *English Traditional Songs and Carols* earlier in 1908. The "Mummers' Carol" begins with a description of the Annunciation that is included in Miss Broadwood's version but is omitted from the one given in the *Oxford Book of Carols* – one wonders why?

At this point special reference should be made to the Journal of 1902 (Vol. 1, No. 4) which is devoted almost wholly to specimens gleaned by Miss Broadwood from Sussex and Surrey about 1892. As the Introduction states – the Journal represents but a very small part of the great quantity of folk-songs that make up her own private collection in order to eliminate those songs which had seen publication before. In the main, the Sussex songs were taken down from a Mr Henry Burstow of Horsham his birth-place, which he avowed at sixty-eight years of age, he had – except for one instance – never left, "not even for a single night". He was in popular demand as a singer both in Sussex and Surrey, and once sang his entire repertory of four hundred songs at the invitation of a gentleman-visitor – a feat that took a full month to accomplish. The Introduction is particularly interesting for its account of the manner in which songs are performed in the Southern Counties. Frequently, the last line of the stanza forms part of the chorus which would then vary from verse to verse. The singers would sing sitting in a rigid posture with their eyes closed, and at the very end of the song the soloist would declaim the final line or the title of the poem in a speaking voice – as an afterthought. As a rule they would perform in the shepherd's white smock-frock that is now becoming such a rarity (cf. *Old English Household Life*, Jekyll and Jones, pl. 127) and most of them could neither read nor write. Here is a new version of the Wassail Song – terminating in the usual cupboard-love – usually associated with the Mummers of West Sussex, particularly Horsham. It was unearthed to the tune "Our Ship She Lies in Harbour" by Alfred Hunt who sent it to Miss Broadwood with a short letter dated 25th April 1905. The melody listed as No. 30 in the above-mentioned Journal is from Surrey where it was sung by a Mr Sparks of Dunsfold in 1896. Mr Cooper another Dunsfold singer invariably preferred D-natural to D-sharp in the second bar:

Ex:20
OUR SHIP SHE LIES IN HAR - BOUR, JUST REA - DY TO SET
SAIL. MAY HEA-VEN BE YOUR GUARD-IAN, LOVE, TILL I RE-TURN FROM SEA.

Joseph and his Wedded Wife
Together as they met
Betwixt them both they never shall part
How happy they may be.

CHORUS: How happy they may be
Betwixt them both they never shall part
How happy they may be.

No mortal man can remember well
When Christ Our Lord was born
He was Crucified between two Thieves
And crowned with the Thorns.

CHORUS: And crowned with the Thorns
He was Crucified between two Thieves
And crowned with the Thorns.

No mortal man can remember well
When Christ died on the Cross
It was for us and our wickedness
Christ precious blood was lost.

CHORUS: Christ precious blood was lost
It was for us and our wickedness
Christ precious blood was lost.

No mortal man can remember well
When Christ was wrapped in Clay
He was buried in some lonesome spot
Where no man then never lay.

CHORUS: Where no man then never lay
He was buried in some lonesome spot
Where no man then never lay.

God bless the Master of this House
His Cattle and his Store
Whether he does walk or whether he does ride
Lord Jesus be his Guide.

CHORUS: Lord Jesus be his Guide
Whether he does walk or whether he does ride
Lord Jesus be his Guide.

God bless the Mistress of this House
With the Gold all on her Breast
Whether she's asleep or whether she's awake
Lord send her soul to rest.

CHORUS: Lord send her soul to rest
Whether she's asleep or whether she's awake
Lord send her soul to rest.

God bless this house and family too
Its Cattle and its store
The Lord will increase you day by day
And send you more and more.

CHORUS: And send you more and more
The Lord will increase you day by day
And send you more and more.

"The Hampshire Mummers' Song" that begins "There is six good days all in a week" was collected by Godfrey Arkwright at Kingsclere in 1897 and appears as No. 20 in this same Journal. It is one of three out of a total of fifty-six that was not actually discovered by Miss Broadwood herself. Although it is of a moralizing nature exhorting parents to bring up their children in the filial fear of God with a pointed reference to the virtue of continence and the eternal consequences of an ill-ordered way of life, like all the songs of the Mummers it partakes of the nature of a Wassail, and with that cheerfulness so characteristic of the friars who always mixed the fearsome with the frolicsome, calls for ale and good cheer in the interests of brotherly love and Christian good-fellowship:

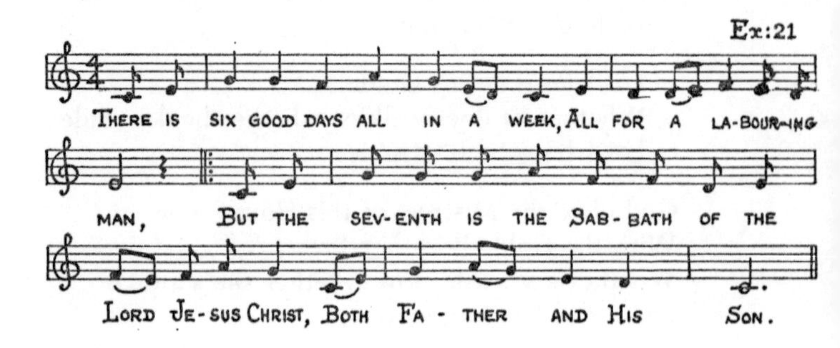
Ex:21
THERE IS SIX GOOD DAYS ALL IN A WEEK, ALL FOR A LA-BOUR-ING
MAN, BUT THE SEV-ENTH IS THE SAB-BATH OF THE
LORD JE-SUS CHRIST, BOTH FA - THER AND HIS SON.

On Sunday go to church, dear man,
Down on our knees we must fall,
And then we must pray that the Lord Jesus Christ
He will bless and save us all.

Bring up your children well, dear man,
Whilst they are in their youth,
For it might be the better for your sweet soul,
When you go to the Lord Jesus Christ.

Now the fields there are as green as green,
As green as any leaf,
Our Lord our God He has watered them
With the heavenly dew so sweet.

In hell it is dark, in hell it is dim;
In hell it is full of lies,
And that is the place where all wicked men must go
When they part from the Lord Jesus Christ.

Then take your Bible in your hand
And read your chapter through;
And when the day of Judgment comes,
The Lord remember you.

Then bring us some of your Christmas ale,
And likewise your Christmas beer;
For when another Christmas comes
We may not all be here.

With one stone at your head, oh man,
And another stone at your feet,
Your good deeds and your evil
Will altogether meet.

In 1877 Richard Chope brought out his *Carols for use in Church* with music edited by H. S. Irons, This collection contained one hundred and twelve songs gleaned from all over Europe, and a fascinating "Introduction" by Baring-Gould gives an account of continental customs observed during the Christmas season, and the "Dance of the Seises"[130] performed every year at Seville on the Feast of Corpus Christi. In 1880 *A Garland of Christmas Carols* was issued by R. Robertson of Newcastle in which the carol "All in the Morning" appears for the first time in a printed collection – but without the verses relating to Lent and Easter. Another notable inclusion is "When Chryst was born of Mary fre" – a folk-carol with a Latin burden that is included in Miss Dean-Smith's *A Guide to English Folk-Song Collections*. It was first published by Thomas Wright from the fifteenth-century Harleian MS (5396) but without a tune, and again appears on its own in Robertson's edition, although in-between times it was published to a melody by A. H. Brown, by Bramley and Stainer in 1871. Another interesting item in Robertson's collection – which contains no music – is "The Twelve Joys of Mary" for special use during the twelve days of the festive season – the forerunner of another folk-song "The Twelve Days of Christmas" to be printed from a Newcastle broadside two years later by Bruce and Stokoe in *Northumbrian Minstrelsy* of 1882.

In 1883 a spectacular little work was published by Charlotte Sophia Burne called *Shropshire Folk-Lore* in which the author discusses not only country customs and traditional beliefs but also the Morris Dance, "The Dancer's Play", and a number of children's games. She gives a number of carol texts some of which are assigned a tune noted from the country-folk, but usually the music is not of a very high quality. The folk-carol "Here we come a-wassailing", the folk-ballad "All under the leaves", two carolites "Sunny Bank" and "While Shepherds Watched" – both folk-songs, are among the specimens included in the collection. In 1893 the words and music of the folk-ballad "The Miraculous Harvest" was noted from oral communication by Lucy Broadwood from some gypsies by the name of Goby. The ballad is a roughly hewn product very similar in form to "The Cherry Tree Carol" discovered by Cecil Sharp in America; it is found in many variants, and its train of thought is broken and confused, with apocryphal references to the

Sojourn in Egypt preserving in its own way what is often lost in the refined and scholarly poem.

The year 1903 saw the publication of *A Garland of Old Castleton Carols* produced and edited by the Rev. W. H. Shawcross, vicar of Bretforton in Worcestershire. This collection, published at the request of the Castleton Parish Choir, gives the texts only of eleven poems; it then mentions a book of carols issued by Richard Kele in 1550 and claims that the songs of the *Castleton Carol Book* are the best and earliest to be found in the district. Among these songs is the very beautiful folk-carol "All in the Morning", thought to have been brought to Derbyshire by some Cornishmen employed in the excavation of the lead-mines about the year 1800. The first verse of this carol as it appears in the *Oxford Book of Carols* and the tune, were taken down by Dr Vaughan Williams from a Mr Hall of Castleton, but the remaining verses are as given in the *Garland* of 1903 by Shawcross, and are the most beautiful of all the texts. This was followed in 1904 by *Nine Songs and Carols* brought out by the Rev. Geoffry Hill, vicar of East and West Harnham in Salisbury, and represented the repertory of a Wiltshire village.

In 1908 Frank Sidgwick issued his *Popular Carols* containing ten specimens which included three folk-ballads "The Bitter Withy", "The Carnal and the Crane", and "The Holy Well"; the three carolites "The Seven Joys", "Adam Lay Ybounden" from the Sloan MS (2593), and "Down in Yon Forest" taken down from oral communication in 1862, and found in *Notes and Queries* started by William Thoms (1803-1885) in 1849. He also includes a version of "Dives and Lazarus" with eighteen verses. In a note at the end of the book the editor writes: "The word 'popular' in the title of this booklet, means that which belongs to the people. These carols therefore are both folk-poetry and demonstrably the traditional property of the people of England. These carols belong to the English "folk". No (writer) could have depicted the childhood of Christ with the homely naïveté of 'The Bitter Withy' and 'The Holy Well' and I for one am convinced that such unwritten and uncanonical lore can never have been regarded throughout the ages of oral tradition with reverence less tender than that bestowed on the New Testament." Some of Sidgwick's beautiful verses with others discovered in Herefordshire are set to a melody from Sandys, and found in No. 56 in the *Oxford Book of Carols*.

Finally, on the very eve of the revival of English national music, we have the publication by Alice Gillington of *Old Christmas Carols from the Southern Counties* in 1910. This collection contains sixteen songs gathered in Surrey, Hampshire, and the New Forest, and although both the texts and the melodies are of indifferent quality, it was the first completely original work to have been published for many years, and the first collection ever to have been noted down purely from oral communication since penal times. This work contains a number of songs and singing games also, many of which have been edited for use in schools; it also gives the very rarely found ballad "In Dessexshire" which tells the legend of the farmer who ploughed on Christmas Day, and "The Twelve Joys of Mary" given in full with the unusual burden – "O the rising of the sun, and the lifting of the day".

In the year 1890, the antiquarian Frank Kidson (d. 1927), whom Lucy Broadwood called "the father of folk-song", published his *Traditional Tunes* which he had gathered while landscape-painting in Yorkshire. A poor man for most of his life, he had spent his days accumulating a vast library of tunes dating from the seventeenth century onwards. About the same time his niece Ethel Kidson published more tunes with a piano accompaniment by Alfred Moffat under the title *Songs of the North Country*. In 1893 *English County Songs* was published by Lucy Broadwood with accompaniments by J. A. Fuller-Maitland, and in the May of 1898 the idea of a society for the preservation of English folk-song was conceived. On 16th June, with Mrs Kate Lee as the principal foundress and Lucy Broadwood as a founder-member, the English Folk-Song Society was formed; and in the February of the following year the first meeting took place with an inaugural address by Sir Hubert

Parry; and the first collection of folk-songs gathered by Kate Lee in Sussex was incorporated in the first issue of the *Journal* which has remained the official organ of the Society ever since. At the death of Mrs Lee in 1904 Lucy Broadwood assumed the rôle of Secretary, and in the same year membership was increased by the arrival of two personages who ever after were to be ranked among the greatest patrons of folk-song – Cecil Sharp and Dr Ralph Vaughan Williams.

Cecil Sharp (1859-1924) is the name best known in the world of folk-song, and it was due to his tireless rummagings in the English countryside[131] and his indefatigable labours among the country folk of the Appalachian mountains of North America[132] that the great revival of English national music was achieved. The two *Journals*, No. 18 and No. 20, which contain among the fifty exhibits a great many carols and chanties collected by Sharp, show just how widespread were his activities. *Journal* No. 6 is devoted entirely to specimens of his own collecting; his scrutiny was always unrelenting and severe, and out of five hundred items collected in the course of three visits to Somerset and North Devon over a period of less than two years, a mere twenty-nine were submitted to the Society. The melodies and texts of many of our favourite Christmas songs as sung at the present time are the result of the individual labours of this one man. In his *English Folk-Carols* published in 1911 there are twenty-one specimens in all – some of which had not previously been published with their tunes. Here in this collection we have a fine version of the "Holly and the Ivy", the verses of which were taken down from a Mrs Clayton at Chipping Campden in Gloucestershire, and supplemented by additional verses from a Mrs Wyatt of East Harptree, Somerset; the poem is set this time, not to the French tune by Rimbault, but to Mrs Clayton's melody by which it is now so well known and loved.[133] The words and music of "On Christmas Night" were noted by Sharp from a Mrs Verrall of Monks Gate, Sussex; "The Somerset Wassail" from the Drayton wassailers of the West Country. "The girt dog of Langport" was thought by Sharp to be a reference to the

Danes whose ravaging of the town is still not forgotten by its inhabitants. Unhappily, however, Cecil Sharp died before he had completed his work. The songs and ballads that make up his *English Folk-Songs* published in two volumes in 1921, all appear in previous collections brought out by him, and a great quantity of songs, ballads, and carols that were to form the ensuing volumes were never published, and still remain inaccessible to the student.

In 1919 Dr Vaughan Williams (1872-1958) published his *Eight Traditional English Carols* which he had noted from oral communication in six different counties – three of the specimens were gathered at Castleton in Derbyshire, where a strong tradition of carol singing has survived to this day. The melody and some verses of the beautiful carolite "The Truth From Above" were noted from a Mr Jenkins of Kings Pyon in Herefordshire; the tune and the entire six verses of "Down in Yon Forest" were taken down from a Mr Hall at Castleton; the melody and five verses of "A May Carol" came from Mr Flack of Fowlmere in Cambridgeshire. An equally valuable collection appeared in 1920 when Dr Vaughan Williams and Ella Leather published their *Twelve Traditional Carols from Herefordshire* which included "The Hereford Carol", for which the tune had been noted from Mr Hirons of Haven, Dilwyn, and the verses from Mr Gallet of Leigh Linton in Worcestershire, from Mr Hirons, and from a ballad sheet published by a Mr Elliot of Hereford. The names of most of these carols appear in previous collections, and the texts were often amended to make their performance the more easy – from *A Good Christmas Box*, and from the collections of Sandys and Silvester.

However, not all of our carols that are now so popular were discovered in the underworld of living folk-song; some had been found in disused manuals hidden away in the dust and lumber of organ lofts, others had lain dormant for generations in manuscript form. "Lullay my Liking", "Wolcum Yole", and the tune of "The Salutation Carol" were all preserved in the fifteenth-century Sloan MS (2593); "Make we Joy" a carol from Southern England dating from the mid-fifteenth century, was printed from the Selden MS (B.26) although the original tune seems to have been lost. Both the words and the music of "What Tidings Messenger" were published by Fuller-Maitland and Rockstro from the Cambridge MS (T.C.C., 0.3.58) in *English Carols from the Fifteenth Century*. The "Souling Song" was published from Playford's *Dancing Master*, and two of the most beautiful carolites ever written – "Adam lay Ybounden" and "I Sing of a Maiden" were reproduced from the Sloan MS but unfortunately without the music. "The Yeoman's Carol" and "The Gallery Carol" – which is not a carol in the strict sense – were both discovered in an old church-gallery song book by the Dorsetshire vicar Rev. L. J. Darwall, and the carolite "Remember O thou Man" was published from Ravencroft's *Melismata*.

The revival of the English carol was accomplished within the greater revival of national music generally, and it soon became universally recognized that England, which was thought to be alone among nations in not having a repertory of national music, had the finest songs of all. With the publication of the *Oxford Book of Carols* in 1928, a wealth of glorious specimens became available to choirmasters throughout the land. Every season of the year has its carols proper to the occasion[134]: the "Furry Day Carol" is a song for ferial days or fair days and was sung throughout Hertfordshire and Huntingdonshire in the course of "luck-visits". The "Psalm of Sion" is a carolite based on the hymn "Jerusalem" by Saint Augustine, and although undoubtedly a great favourite on "Mothering Sunday" it is an item that may be sung at any time. However, of all our carols it is those in praise of Christmas that are the most numerous and have the most vigorously survived, and it is due to the interest and industry not only of scholars and collectors of folk-song, but of country parsons and of the parson-squire,[135] that carol singing, as heard at Christmas time in the cathedrals and churches of our land, is now one of the most glorious experiences of the year.[136] Moreover, our repertory of Christmas carols is a common inheritance in which the man in the street and the University professor are equally at home; they are above all a social possession, and the singing of these simple songs invariably has the wholesome if rather startling effect of reducing all men to the same common denominator as children of one great human family. There would seem to be no more practical way of uniting Christians of different religious beliefs than by the communal singing of carols at Christmas time.[137] God who became incarnate, who lived and died for the human race, has left us an international repertory of folk-song through which the nations of the earth with a common voice, can express their love in return. In fine, carols are a simple and popular expression of Christian belief in which all can share, and a welcome relaxation from the tumult of twentieth-century everyday life. The carol, as fresh now as ever brings us the peace of mediaeval England, and today, above the din of national conflict, in a world beset with fear and uncertainty as to the future, comes the message of the carol, sweet and serene:

Love and joy come to you,
And to you your wassail too,
And God bless you, and send you
A happy new year,
And God send you a happy new year.[138]

Chapter 6

The Folk-Carol Today

In the first chapter of his *English Folk-Song* (p. 5) Cecil Sharp remarks that the real antithesis between art-song and folk-song lies not so much in the difference between town and country as between the skilled and unskilled artist. Accordingly, many present-day students of folk-song subscribe to the view that is gaining in popularity, that true folk-song is in no way incompatible with modern industrial society, and that genuine specimens are to be found wherever there is a sizeable community of workmen whose artistic faculties have undergone no formal training. An article by John Handle on this subject appeared in an issue of *English Dance and Song* published from Cecil Sharp House in the August of 1965 which included a folk-carol gleaned in recent years from a colliery district in the North-East. We give it here as it was noted down by W. Toyne from a Mr Natress of Low Fell, Gateshead, who learnt it from his grandfather Mr Jonas Natress of the Hetton District Collieries:

BURDEN: Jowl! Jowl! and listen lad
And hear the coal face workin',
There's many a marra missin' lad
Becaas he wadn't listen lad.

STANZA: Me feyther aalwes used to say
That pit wark's mair than hewin'

Ye've got te coax the coal alang
And not just rivin and tewin so!

Noo the deppity craals from flat te flat
While the putter rams the tuum 'uns.
But the man at the face hes te knaa his place
Like a mother knaas hor young 'uns so!

There is no doubt whatsoever that this specimen is a genuine folk-carol; nevertheless many collectors – perhaps the majority – would feel that they could not subscribe to this view except perhaps in those rare instances where a vigorous corporate and family relationship existed among the workers who responded to a natural impulse that was spontaneous and independent of subversive political influence.

It is true to say that after his Christian religion, the most precious possession of the mediaeval peasant was the complete freedom he enjoyed in the use of his time. The tenor of his life was an even and leisurely one: he was born into the tranquillity of village life from which he never stirred; he married in it, lived in it, and died in it. If perforce a journey had to be made, if it was not on foot then it was with the aid of the old hack or cob, or in the case of a longer journey – by stage-coach, transport that was as slow as it was hazardous. The peasant's time was his own; he had plenty of it, and he used it as and when he pleased. He was never in a hurry. Moreover, he was first and foremost a community-man and his relationship with the village community and its common interests was as closely interlocked as oxen with plough, and plough with earth. He worked not for an overlord but solely for himself and the village. It was in such an age of peace and security that our English folk-song took shape, and the time factor was the soil in which it thrived.

The bitter enemy of folk-song is speed. With the arrival of the Industrial Revolution and the widespread use of machinery culminating in the invention and development of the internal combustion engine, the traditional pattern of English life began to change; the working man surrendered his independence, and with it the right to call his time his own. What we now inelegantly refer to as "the rat-race" began in reality not in the twentieth but in the eighteenth century, and with the increase in poverty and unemployment, man became so preoccupied with his own prospects of survival and means of livelihood that understandably, he had no time to devote to the community as a whole. An anti-social insularity was the result. In modern industrial society where for many people even Sunday is no longer a day of rest, the pace of life is so fast that people no longer have either the time or the incentive to contribute towards their own recreation. At the end of a hard day's work, a man on arriving home weary from the endless queueings and the rush-hour traffic is in no condition to provide his own entertainment! Consequently, not only the old labour-rhythms and "waulking-songs" but community singing and even the piano itself have in most cases disappeared from the home and given place to the radio, the television, and the record-player. We live in an age of mechanized entertainment of which the "Juke-Box" is perhaps the ugliest example. Gilbert Keith Chesterton (1874-1936) in one of his "Songs of Education" has compared the old with the new and given us food for thought in a well known satire – this surely is not the climate in which folk-song can flourish:

O Warwick woods are green, are green,
But Warwick trees can fall;
And Birmingham grew so big, so big,
And Stratford stayed so small.
Till the hooter howled to the morning lark
That sang to the morning star;
And we all became, in freedom's name,
The fortunate chaps we are.

The fortunate chaps, the felicitous chaps,
The fairy-like chaps we are.

The people they left the land, the land,
But they went on working hard;

And the village green that had got mislaid
Turned up in the squire's back-yard;
But twenty men of us all got work
On a bit of his motor car;
And we all became with the world's acclaim,
The marvellous mugs we are.

The marvellous mugs, miraculous mugs,
The mystical mugs we are.

Within the last decade a competition was launched by the *Sunday Times* in which readers were invited to compose the text of a Christmas carol in a twentieth-century idiom. Many hundreds of entries were received by the adjudicator of which a good proportion were of a high artistic standard. After the adjudicator had decided upon the winning entry he assessed the merits of the compositions in his summing up:

> The entries unfolded into a newsreel of images of our time. The compounds, the barbed wire, the sentries stamping in the cold, the mobs, the rockets pointing to the heavens – all the sad paraphernalia of the peace which is not peace surrounded the Christ child. The scarred places of injustice recurred again and again, from Budapest to Capetown; and, much more often than anywhere else, Notting Hill Gate – as if the sordid and the fearful were ultimately more of an insult to God than the dramatically terrible. Yet the note of hope was not lacking, not only because of the significance of the Incarnation, but because D.P. camps, railway stations and places like Notting Hill were seen as spots where a twentieth-century Mary and her Child could find friendly succour, comradeship and compassion.

The following is an extract from a contribution submitted by Elizabeth Carnegy; it was typical of many such entries:

Next door a baby cries. All's still.
Christ is here in Notting Hill.
Steel band and Calypso sing
Christ is born to be our king.

The joyousness of the event whatever the circumstances, was a realization that dominated most of the entries in an attempt to offer a homely welcome to the Incarnate Godhead who had laid aside His grandeur to dwell among us. Here is part of the entry submitted by A. V. Clarke:

I'm going to see the baby, Jack
Whether you come with me or not.
I've left your dinner in the oven hot
And I'm going to see the baby.

The prize-winning entry was contributed by a Mr R. F. Colvile and was aptly described by the adjudicator as – "something very ordinary, very twentieth-century, and very near to home, but very gracious":

CHILD OF OUR TIME

BURDEN: Stay! O stay! good travellers all, for God is born a Man
And lies wrapped in a table-cloth within a railway van.

STANZA: Joseph came to Somers Town, behind the Euston Road
Evicted from his caravan and now of no abode;
Mary sought a lodging there, shelter for her head,
But all the jostling houses could offer them no bed.

So Mary came to Euston, where a porter found them room
In a shunted unused guard's van half shrouded in the gloom.

And there with no possessions, no midwife standing by,
There rang throughout the station her new-born baby's cry.

The porters came and wished her luck and brought them cups of tea
And as the rumour spread around there came to Platform Three
The other weary travellers, who travelled Christmas Day,
And offered Him a tribute, then turned and went their way.

It is worth noting before entertaining any hope of a reappearance of the folk-composition among the industrial classes, that although it is ten years since the competition took place, not one of all the many hundreds of specimens specially written for the occasion has been either seen or heard of since. Had they been written in the fourteenth or fifteenth century they would by now have become an invaluable part of our folk-carol repertory. So far as I am aware, no tune has yet been found for this very beautiful and poignant Christmas carol, and the author has rescued it from oblivion to include it in these pages with a burden of his own composing, in the hope that one day, a composer will see his way to providing the music for these twentieth-century verses.

APPENDIX

A TWENTIETH-CENTURY CAROL

(by Sydney Carter) (E.F.D.S.S.)

BURDEN: God above, man below, Holy is the name I know.

STANZA: Every star shall sing a carol
Every creature high and low,
Come and praise the king of heaven
By whatever name you know.

When the king of all creation
Had a cradle on the Earth,
Holy was the human body
And the day that gave him birth.

Who can tell what other cradle
High above the Milky Way
Still may rock the king of heaven
On another Christmas Day?

Who can tell how many crosses,
Still to come or long ago,
Crucify the king of Heaven?
Holy is the name I know.

Every creature he will gather,
All shall know him for their own.
I will praise the son of Mary,
Brother of my blood and bone.

Every star and every planet,
Every creature high or low,
Sing the everlasting carol:
Holy is the name I know.

A TWENTIETH-CENTURY CAROL

(by Honourable Mrs Addington) 1952

BURDEN: Sleep, oh my son, that may not sleep again!
Upon our earth the Prince of Peace is born
Who brings us but the sword – and Herod's men
Steal through the shambas with their long knives drawn.

STANZA: My son, the God of heaven has a Son
No bigger than thou art; and silently
His Mother rocks His cot when day is done,
And watches Him even as I watch thee.

Sleep, little one, that shall not wake again!
Across the way the Prince of Peace is born
Who brings us but the sword – and Herod's men
Steal through the alleys with their long knives drawn

His Mother shall arise before the day
And flee with Him far out of Bethlehem;
And there, unknown and exiled, shall He stay –
The promised King who built Jerusalem.

And when He shall return unto His own
Thy brethren shall spit upon His head,
And claim the pagan Caesar for the throne,
And curse themselves, and shout to see Him dead.

Sleep, little one, that shall not wake again!
Across the way the Prince of Peace is born
Who brings us but the sword – and Herod's men
Steal among the bundu with their long knives drawn

But when through all the ages they shall sing
Of how the Lord of heaven sent His Son
And how the people did not know their king
Then shall they sing of thee, my little one!

Then shall they sing the Holy Innocents
Who from bright heaven, amongst the cherubim,
Beg Him to turn His eyes from our offence
Who have not known, who have not cherished Him.

This beautiful "Lullaby" was written in Kenya shortly before Christmas and at the outbreak of the Mau Mau rebellion of 1952. It was inspired by the tragic suffering that accompanied the insurrection and the annihilation of an entire Christian community near Nyeri on Boxing Day of the same year. In this instance many children were brutally mutilated. In a communication from the author herself, it was stated that the message of the carol was that however much we may sympathize with the ultimate purpose of the organization, the Oathtaking Ceremony and the beastliness of its campaign rendered the movement incompatible with Christian teaching.

A TWENTIETH-CENTURY CAROL

(by John Forest) 1966 q.v. Index

BURDEN: Lets all go to Bethlehem
It isn't very far,
We can all go together
In daddy's motorcar.

STANZA: There's the way to Bethlehem –
Over on the right;
We're sure to find the manger
If we follow that bright light!

We'll fill the car with loads of sweets
And lots and lots of toys;
But when we get there, mummy says –
We mustn't make a noise!

On and on, and on we went,
As fast as we could go,
All through the night – where were we? –
Even daddy didn't know.

On we went, but slower now
Across the virgin snow,
When suddenly – we knew not how –
The car was all aglow.

The star was now right overhead
Although we did not know;
We stopped, and one by one got out,
So gently – on tip-toe.

We stood before the stable door –
It had been left ajar –
Will the Holy Infant know
We've come so very far?

We tip-toed in across the straw
With fruit and sweets and all,
And placed them at the tiny feet
Before the oxen's stall.

The Maiden raised her eyes and smiled,
Her face so full of joy:
She was so pleased that we had come
To see her little Boy.

We knelt awhile; then left for home –
Through palm and fir and oak,
And all the way from Bethlehem
No single word we spoke.

A TWENTIETH-CENTURY CAROL

(by Margaret Marshall) 1964

BURDEN: Three in one, and one in three,
(q. v. Index) Hail the Holy Trinity

Fountain-head of unity
Father of the family.

STANZA: Mary, Joseph, little son,
Three in one, and one in three,
God's own pattern for the world,
Blesséd be this trinity.

Father, mother, newborn babe,
Three in one, and one in three,
Blest the parents, blest the child,
Blesséd be this trinity.

Father, Son, and Holy Ghost,
Three in one, and one in three,
Thou the living centre be,
Of each growing family.

A TWENTIETH-CENTURY CAROL

(by Joseph Marshall) 1955

BURDEN: God is with us from above:
(q. v. Index) Born a man to die of love.
His a bed of stable straw,
Love he needs and nothing more.

STANZA: Christ is born: an infant boy.
Alleluia! Shout for joy!
Death had come through Adam's fall:
Life has come to grace us all.

Christ of all the world is King:
Gaudeamus! Let us sing!
Give him hearts no longer cold –
So bring royal gift of gold.

Christ is God – though truly man:
Jubilemus all we can!
Prayers rise as sweetest scents –
Gift of God is frankincense,

Christ himself Redeemer came –
Felix culpa! – spurning shame.
God forgives but – do not err –
Penance sharp is gift of myrrh.

Christ has come to ask our love:
Diligamus God above!
Let us love him – you and me –
Now and in eternity.

A TWENTIETH-CENTURY BALLAD

(by Honourable Mrs Addington) 1940

"I Saw Three Ships come sailing by"

(1) I saw a ship with satin sails
And masts of solid gold;
There were comforts in the cabin
And apples in the hold.

And on the deck the captain stood
And called for all to hear:
"Oh men and women of the world
Oh monied men, come here!

Behold the halls and marble pools
And decks for your delight
Swaying with flowers and flags by day
And fairy-lights by night!

Come listen to the melodies
That woo you without cease;
Or in the cushioned cabins play
With love, or take your ease!

My table serves a royal fare,
My cellars lyric wine.
There's nothing in the earth or sky –
Not a thing that gold can buy
That lacks this ship of mine."

"Captain," I said, "Oh captain,
Where does your fine ship go?"
But like a wistful child he sighed:
"Alas, I do not know."

(2) I saw a great grey battleship
With masts of flaring steel.
She smote the wind and carved the sea
That cowered at her keel.

And on the deck the captain stood
And called for all to hear:
"Oh men of spirit, modern men,
Oh brave new men, come here!

No more shall false allegiances
Enslave you as of old;
For they that clasped the ancient creeds
Lie fettered in the hold.

Their wives have no more eyes to weep,
Their babes no light to see;
And they shall envy skeletons
That rattle in the sea.

But all the rest with single hand
Shall man the decks along;
And from a single heart shall surge
A dedicated song.

Tireless and proud their toil shall be,
Holy their fellowship;
And even in their yearning dreams
Nought see they but the ship."

"Oh iron captain" questioned I,
"Where does your journey end?"
He said "There is no more to seek:
The ship is all, my friend."

(3) I saw a ship, a little ship
Sail like the crescent moon;
And at the helm there sat a girl
Singing a cradle tune.

But though she lulled a tiny child
Great was her majesty;
And all the flowers and all the stars
Were not as fair as she.

Oh keep your grimness and your gold,
For right across the sky
We'll sail until we reach the land;
She, the Child, and I.

For wealth is dry and men must die,
But still our day is dawning –
I saw a ship come sailing by
On Christmas Day in the morning!

A TWENTIETH-CENTURY CAROL

(by Peter Jackson) 1966 q.v. Index

BURDEN: Red and yellow, black and white,
Golden talent, widow's mite,
All are men of equal right
As creatures, in God's holy sight.

STANZA: I'm going to see the Baby, Bill,
He's with us here, in Notting Hill:
See how the air a silence fills!
This is a wondrous matter.

I'll bake a custard, dainty, light,
And take some blankets soft and white
To save them from the cold at night.
These people really matter.

With beauty laden, sweetly proud,
Stealing gangway through the crowd,
A slattern laughs and calls aloud . . .
  Forget it; end the matter!

What colour was the fellow's skin
The portly keeper of the inn
Who bawled: "Outside! – no room within!"
  It doesn't really matter.

Give the poor but a drink of tea
And what you do, you do to Me,
The Master said in Galilee.
  Poppycock and chatter!

Her hour had come; no more to roam,
In Notting Hill she found a home
In a disused air-raid catacomb.
  No one thought it mattered.

A Babe was born in Notting Hill
To save us from eternal ill;
Unwelcomed and unwanted still.
  Nothing seems to matter.

Was she black or was she white
That brought Him forth on Christmas night
The Lord of Darkness and of Light?
  It surely doesn't matter.

Was it some Calypso tune
She crooned to hush her little coon
Beneath a grey suburban moon?
  Love is all that matters.

I've been across to Notting Hill –
I left your dinner on the grill –
It's burnt down to a cinder Bill?
  But does it really matter?

A TWENTIETH-CENTURY SUSSEX CAROL

(by Peter Jackson) September 1966 q. v. Index

BURDEN: Most wonderful of wondrous things:
A maiden bears the King of Kings.

STANZA: The face of heaven itself beheld
The place where He was born,
And with her blushes woke the hills
To welcome him at dawn.

"My morning sheen I have from thee,
Of radiance I have none;
And in my lowliness I greet
The Sun-lit and the Sun.

I'll bid the chattering brook be still,
(He has so much to say!)
And tell him of the joyful news,
And that it's Christmas Day!"

"A silent wonder fills the air,
I feel it in my stones;
My fishes feel it in their gills
And in their very bones!"

I'll crown her hair with morning light
And tint her cheeks with red,
And touch the gentle straw that holds
His hands and feet and head.

I'll peep within her mantle folds
Where none but He doth know,
And tip the virgin caps that raise
Two cherries in the snow.

I shall not wake the woolly lambs
That sleep within the fold:
They and the shepherds heard the news
Ere even I was told.

Annotated Bibliography

Chapter 1

1 Henry Ramsden Bramley, *Christmas Carols New and Old*, 1871.
2 *Early English Christmas Carols*, 1961. Introduction, p. 2.
3 *A Collection of Old Christmas Carols, with the Tunes to which they are sung, chiefly traditional*, 1863.
4 Preface, p. v.
5 *Everyman's Dictionary of Music*, 1946.
6 *Oxford Companion to Music.*
7 Chap. viii, p. 124.
8 *The English Carol*, p. 25.
9 *The Early English Carol*, 1935, Preface, p. xxiii.
10 *The New Oxford History of Music*, Vol. iii, chap. iv, p. 121.
11 Pages lviii and cxxv.
12 The Latin songs referred to here may all be found in the *Liber Usualis* a manual containing the official music of the Roman Rite and the possession of every presbytery.
13 *The Month*, October 1949; *Music and the Liturgy*, p. 261.
14 Grimm believes that "troubadour" is derived from the German "treffen" through the Gothic "drupan".
15 Douglas Brice, *The Downside Review*, *Trope and Sequence*, April 1962.
16 The female troubadour did exist; but she was not common.
17 "In all his maze of multitudinous words, in all his wandering paths of narrative meditation, in all the thousand things that he touches on as a poet, a philosopher, a moralist and a humorist, he has not left one single word which throws any light on those political missions which the King his master trusted to him to conduct with the princes of France and the great merchants of Italy. A little is known about the subject of some of his journeys abroad, but there are others that seem to have been of the Secret Service that is really secret." G. K. C., *Chaucer*, p. 95.

18 It is interesting to note that the Flagellants made a brief appearance in England during the reign of Edward III (1327-1377) but without success. cf Lingard, *History of England*, Vol. III. chap. II, p. 159.

19 The word "stanza" is thought to be derived from the Latin "stare" meaning "to remain stationary".

20 Greene, *The Early English Carol*, CXXI.

21 *Saint Francis of Assisi*, chap. III, p. 41, *passim.*

22 *The Franciscans and the Carol.*

23 CXXII.

24 Idem, CCXII.

25 *Saint Francis of Assisi*, p. 14, *passim.*

26 It is our considered opinion that in an age when the rank and file of our society know so little of God, and are so unfamiliar with the teaching of Christ – not merely an interest, but a serious study, and a genuine love of the carol is absolutely imperative in any clergyman to whatsoever denomination he may subscribe, devoted to the instruction of the English people.

27 *The Early English Carol*, CVIII, *passim.*

28 *English Folk-Song*, chap. VIII, p. 125.

29 The style of this beautiful polyphony, with its quaint submediant-to-tonic flavour would suggest that it belongs to the "Ars Nova" period and the age of Dunstable.

30 *Music of the Catholic Church*, chap. IV, p. 79.

31 *Music in Mediaeval Britain*, chap. VII, p. 417, footnote.

32 CXXVII.

33 Manfred Bukofzer, *The New Oxford History of Music*, Vol. III, chap. IV, p. 118.

34 *The New Oxford History of Music*, Vol. III, chap. VII, p. 250.

35 *Chaucer*, chap. VI, p. 189.

36 The age of chivalry, that is to say – the age of the English carol is personified in the character of Geoffrey Chaucer: "Chaucer certainly did not hate women, let alone lovers; he did not hate anybody. All his talents were on the side of sympathy. In the 'Legend of Good Women' he praised each woman in turn for being a faithful lover. But he could not bring himself to curse a woman, even for being a false lover. The curious way in which this corner is turned, with a curve rather than an angle, is one of the most singular and individual qualities in the poem that probably he wrote most carefully and seriously, and intended

to be the outstanding creation of his career." G. K. C., *Chaucer*, chap. IV, p. 141.

Chapter 2

37 R. L. Greene. *The Early English Carol*, IVIII.
38 Shane Leslie, *An Anthology of Catholic Poets*, 1925.
39 *English Folk-Song*, chap. I, p. 4.
40 Among German students, the term "folk-song" is meant to include a large percentage of national songs that in England would be rejected as "popular songs". Both Haydn and Beethoven wrote variations on English and Scottish folk-songs that have now been discarded by Cecil Sharp and his followers as "popular songs" composed by the skilled musician of the town.
41 Beatrice Blackwood, *Ethnology, Folk-Lore, and Popular Art*, p. 89, cf. *Journal*, No. 3, Vol. IV, December 1942.
42 Wilfrid Mellers, *Music and Society*, chap. I, p. 20.
43 The tune of "Auld Lang Syne" came originally from France, and is still sung today to the text of "Chant de l'unité". It is probable that a Calvinist brought the hymn to Scotland where the verses were discarded and a poor text put in its place. In 1945, David Sleigh of Banff, Scotland, heard forty children of all colours at a convent school in Malaya, sing "Auld Lang Syne" in Chinese, but the verses were those of the hymn:

> Restons toujours unis, mes frères
> Si nous nous aimons tous
> Comme il nous a promis, mes frères,
> Si nous nous aimons tous.

44 Gustave Reese, *Music in the Middle Ages*, p. 160.
45 Knud Jeppeson, *The Polyphonic Vocal Style of the Sixteenth Century*, p. 68.
46 Cf. "Liber Usualis", In Nativitate Domini, Ad Primam Missam in Nocte. It is noticeable that in the chant setting for the Communion of this Mass the intervals Me-Fah, and Te-Doh are entirely absent.
47 Chap. 2, p. 12.
48 C. Sharp, *English Folk-Song*, chap. 8, pp. 113 and 114.

49 Idem, p. 114.
50 R. L. Greene, *The Early English Carol*, LVIII.
51 *Studies in Literature*, p. 33.
52 The "a" vowel coincided with an unaccented note at the end of a tune. Always the easiest vowel upon which to vocalize, it recalls the Alleluia and the jubilus in the age of the trope.
53 Anne Gilchrist, *Journal*, Vol. 5, No. 1, December 1946, p. 35.
54 The following versions of "The Three Kings of Cologne" and its derivative "I Saw Three Ships", with the observations that accompany them, are taken from the contributions of Anne Gilchrist to *Journal*, No. 1, Vol. v, December 1946.
55 Article with musical illustration: "The Cherry Tree Ballad", The Times Library, 23rd December 1955.
56 Cecil Sharp, *English Folk-Songs from the Southern Appalachians.*
57 H. E. Piggott, *Journal*, No. 20, Vol. 5, part 3, p. 323. November 1916.
58 *Journal*, No. 14, Vol. IV, June 1910.
59 "The ball-play episode seems to borrow its formula from the ballad of 'Little Sir Hugh', and it seems possible that, besides the Luccan fresco and the old French references to chastisement, 'the little rod under her apron' with which Sir Hugh's mother goes out to find her boy who has tarried too long, may have helped to suggest the beating. Compare the curious tag at the end of Motherwell's 'Sir Hugh':

> 'O the broom, the bonny bonny broom,
> The broom that makes full sore;
> A woman's mercy is very little,
> But a man's mercy is more.'"

Journal, No. 14, Vol. 4, June 1910 – Anne Gilchrist.
60 Pseudo-James, chap. XVII, verse 7; chap. XV, verses 3 and 4; chap. XIX, verses 9, 12, 16-24. Cf. Frances Fox, *Legends of the Christ Child*, Sheed and Ward, 1942.
61 Pseudo-Thomas, chap. 2, verses 1-9.
62 Anne Gilchrist, *Journal*, No. 14, 1st part of Vol. 4, June 1910.
63 3954 fol. 70, fourteenth century; 2399 fol. 47, fifteenth century.
64 Lucy Broadwood, *Journal*, No. 30, the fifth part of Vol. 7, August 1926, p. 285. Note also the painting "Madonna and Child with Saints" by Sebastian Schel (1479-1554).

65 For a study of the "lingua franca" of folk-song, cf. James Reeves, *The Everlasting Circle*, p. 21; *The Idiom of the People*, p. 45.
66 Frank Kidson, *Journal*, No. 20, Vol. 5, part 3, p. 279, November 1916. The present writer was dependent upon the notes in this *Journal* for his account.
67 *Henry IV*, Part 2, Act 2, Scene 4, The Boar's Head Tavern, Eastcheap, London.

Chapter 3

68 "Nullus in festivitate S. Joannis, vel quibuslibet sanctorum solemnitatibus solstitia aut ballationes vel saltationes aut caraulas aut cantica diabolica exerceat." *St Ouen's Life of St Eligius*, II, 15. Cf. *The Folk-Carol*, *The Month*, November 1959, p. 272, footnote.
69 The following is an example of the abuse which sometimes affected the liturgical drama of the period: "The feast of the ass, celebrated annually at Beauvais on 14th January was a dramatisation of the flight into Egypt. A girl, carrying an infant gorgeously dressed, processed from the cathedral to the church of St Etienne. Entering the choir, she took up a position before the altar – still riding the ass. Mass was celebrated in the course of which the words 'Hin han' were chanted in imitation of the bray." Cf. *The Folk-Carol*, *The Month*, November 1959, p. 273, footnote.
70 Anyone with any experience of English audiences will know that vociferous outbursts whether of applause or disapproval are the normal thing.
71 W. J. Phillips, *Carols, their origin and connection with the Mystery Play*, p. 21.
72 Idem, p. 105.
73 Idem.
74 Frank Harrison, *Music in Mediaeval Britain*, p. 417.
75 Luke, chap. 23, verse 31.
76 Anne Gilchrist, *Journal of the English Folk-Song Society*, No. 14, 1910, p. 52.
77 R. L. Greene, *The Early English Carol*, chap. IV, XCIV.
78 Anne Gilchrist, *Journal*, 1910. It should be emphasized that but for the researches of this eminent scholar there would have

been little that was reliable available on the subject of this carol.

79 Anne Gilchrist, *Journal of English Folk-Song*, December 1942, Vol. 4, No. 3, p. 122.

80 The Epiklesis was a prayer invoking the Holy Spirit. It is interesting to observe that as part of the modern liturgical movement the hymn "Veni Sancte Spiritus" is now being sung by the entire congregation immediately following the Offertory prayer.

81 Luke, chap. 22, verse 12.

82 It should be remembered that in the fourteenth and fifteenth centuries church ritual throughout almost the entire British Isles was the luxuriant Sarum ceremonial introduced into this country by Richard le Poore (1217-1228).

83 *Journal*, June 1910, No. 14, Vol. 4, 1st part, p. 65.

84 *Journal*, January 1914, No. 18, Vol. 5, 1st part, p. 20.

85 Idem.

86 Idem, p. 21.

87 This carol otherwise known as "The New Forest Carol", was obtained for the present author by Margaret Dean-Smith, 16th June 1965.

88 James Reeves, *The Everlasting Circle*, Introduction, chap. 6. "The Lingua Franca" derives from prior concept and discussion of Miss Margaret Dean-Smith.

89 *The Oxford Book of Carols*, 1953, No. 183.

90 Lucy Broadwood is of the opinion that "gold rings" might possibly be a corruption of the Scottish "goldspinks" or "goldfinches"; if not, then a derivation of "gulderer" or "gulder-cock" meaning "turkey" – the turkey being common in French versions of the carol where 'gold-ring' often appears as a species of bird. Cf. *Journal*, November 1916, No. 20, Vol. 5, part 3, p. 280.

91 Lucy Broadwood found that the more usual method of performing this carol was "to begin with the 'twelfth day', and in subsequent verses to omit one day at a time in reversed numerical order until the second day is reached; then the process is reversed, the days added one by one till the singer reaches the verse he began with."

92 Cecil Sharp, *English Folk-Song*, chap. 8, p. 124.

93 Luke, chap. 2, verses 8-14. "The Wakefield Christmas Play" performed annually in Yorkshire in mediaeval times would seem to indicate that the English country-folk were by no means as illiterate as we have been led to believe. A peasantry with a

knowledge of "The Five Species of Counterpoint" can hardly be called illiterate!

FIRST SHEPHERD: Say what was his song?
Heard ye not how he cracked it?
Three breves to a long?

SECOND SHEPHERD: Yea, marry, he hacked it,
Was no crotchet wrong
Nor no thing that lacked it!

This choir would have obviously swept the board at any festival!

Chapter 4

94 *The "Adeste Fideles" – a Study on Its Origin and Development*, 1947, "Publications", Buckfast Abbey, South Devon.

95 "Acknowledgement must be made to the Reverend Father Rector of Conglowes Wood College, Kildare, who tried to help by searching for the Wade MS of the Adeste, which had been in possession of the College for perhaps two hundred years, but has recently 'been lost or stolen' from the Library. This was sad news indeed, as the Conglowes copy was always given pride of place as the earliest known!" – *The "Adeste Fideles" – A Study*, Introduction p. 4, 1.

96 Erik Routley and Professor Robbins both accept the findings of Dom John Stéphan which are now no longer held in question.

Chapter 5

97 Francis Gasquet, "*Henry VIII and the English Monasteries*", Vol. 2, chap. 10, p. 423. "The purchasers of the houses used the MSS for every vile and common necessity." "Grocers and soap-sellers" bought them for their business purposes. While one merchant bought "the contents of two noble libraries for forty shillings price", and "this stuff hath he occupied instead of grey paper" adds the author, "by the space of more than these ten years: and yet he hath store enough for as many years to come."

Sir Richard Terry, *The Music of the Roman Rite*, chap. XXVI, p. 217.

For a defence of the puritans, cf. Scholes, *The Puritans and Music*, O.U.P. 1936.

John Harvey, *Gothic England*, 1947, chap. v, p. 109: "Mr Scholes has written a long work to prove that the puritans were not guilty of the excesses against music attributed to them. This is perfectly true, and yet, we cannot disguise the fact that England has been relatively indifferent to all forms of art during the past four centuries."

98 Tract, pub. 1656. A presbyterian controversialist who having graduated at Balliol College, Oxford, in 1612, opened a school at Aldermanbury seven years later. He published *Inquiries into the Causes of our Miseries* in 1644, and became vicar of Bray near Maidenhead in 1649. Within ten years he had been expelled.

99 The story is still told in London at Christmas time for the amusement of the young – how the puritan officers would parade the streets and peer through the windows in the discharge of their duty; and how the angry householders would put them to flight before a rain of reject comestibles.

100 Erik Routley, *The English Carol*, 1958, p. 49.

101 Charles Villiers Stanford, *A History of Music*, chap. XII, p. 233.

102 In the Pulborough and Midhurst districts alone, fifty-two folk-songs were noted from oral communication and are included in the *Journal* of the English Folk-Song Society for 1901. Most of the songs in the *Journals* of 1899, 1900, and 1902 are from Sussex also. Songs from the same county were contributed to the *Journal* of 1906 by Dr Vaughan Williams; 1913 by G. S. K. Butterworth; and 1918 by Lady Ashton of Hyde. Cf. Margaret Dean-Smith, *Journal*, 1951, p. 70.

103 Hilaire Belloc, *The Cruise of the "Nona"*, p. 113.

104 *The Cambridge Modern History*, Vol. 6, chap. XXIV, pp. 822 and 824.

105 *The History of Germany*, Vol. 3, CCXLV, p. 152. Professor A. Gillies, *Herder*, 1945. Sir Isaiah Berlin, *Herder*, cf. *Encounter*, July 1965, pp. 29 to 48.

106 His first ambition as a young man was to enter the medical profession, and in 1762 he went to Königsberg where he began a course in surgery under a Russian physician. He fainted at the first sight of dissection and the project was abandoned.

107 It is interesting to compare specimens such as "A Virgin Most Pure", "Here we come a-wassailing", and "The Holly and the

Ivy" with the inelegant "Cherry Tree Ballad" from the Southern Appalachians, which from its allusion to oriental custom would seem to date from the time of the Crusades; and we should not imagine that because a peasantry is uneducated or even non-educated, that therefore it is necessarily uncultured. Folk-song attains its full stature only as handmaid to the Christian religion, and a peasantry that lived in the shadow of the cathedrals and abbeys of pre-Reformation England could not but have imbibed a great deal of mediaeval and Renaissance culture which has remained unrivalled in western Europe even up to the present day. The "folk" of the fifteenth century England would have been an entirely different community from that of a continent which, at a time when Christian culture was at its zenith, had not yet been discovered.

108 This distinction might at first sight appear unreasonable, but not when we reflect that the unprintable supplement to the townsmen's vocabulary would have perplexed the mediaeval peasant as it would have done Chaucer and Langland. It was not after all from the Royalists that the Roundheads met their match in the end, but from "the gypsies in the wood", who living a camouflaged existence away from the centres of puritanism, were able to preserve the ancient faith and a sanity that went with it.

109 Dean-Smith, *A Guide to English Folk-Song Collections*, p. 12.

Particularly interesting are those modern folk-songs brought to this country by refugees from China. Some are peasant songs, others were written by students who had been put to work in the fields. One song tells of how the people were forced to eat weeds on account of the food shortage:

> In farming we exhaust our efforts:
> Weeds from the water cost four cents a catty (per lb.)
> High as the sky is ambition,
> But the wheat is thin as a needle.

Another describes the sufferings of the women-folk whom the State Nurseries have relieved of their babies that they might work in the fields:

> When the wheat is reaped and the threshing done,
> Which girl at leisure does not think of home,

Hoe in hand and tears in eyes,
Yet the platoon commander says:
"You backward devils"!

The Chinese student is so frustrated as to become a victim of despair and on the brink of suicide – "By sea, road and sky":

Before dawn we study, then take picks for loosening the yellow earth.
We yearn for a better life, but waste our six years' time.
– (*preparatory schooling*.)
We collapse with picks in hands,
Yet they say we are attacked by fits.
Looking at the far distance, we find nothing
But sea, road and sky.

110 Idem, p. 13, footnote.

111 "It was Johann Herder unremembered at the present time, who first turned the thoughts of those around him to that natural wild-flower poetry which springs up of itself in every country, and led the way into a new world of thought which others since his time have made their own. Our debt to Herder is that he gave the perception of the worth of common things." Theodora Nunns, "The Sponsor of Folk-Song", Article, *The Temple Bar Journal*, 1897, quoted by Dean-Smith, *Guide*, p. 13.

112 The dilapidated remains of this MS were discovered under a bureau by Thomas Percy (1729-1811) in whose honour the "Percy Society" was founded in 1840 by Thomas Wright and others. The MS which seems to have been kept under lock and key for a hundred years in accordance with strict puritan tradition, contains in addition to a collection of ballads, a fourteenth-century cycle of allegorical poems modelled on *Piers Plowman* entitled *Death and Liffe*. The MS itself was eventually published in 1867 by Hales and Furnivall at the entreaties of the American scholar Francis James Child.

113 James Macpherson a farmer's son, was born at Kingussie and graduated at Edinburgh University. He had outstanding literary ability and a knowledge of Gaelic poetry. In 1763 in the company of several Highland gentlemen, he published his *Temora*, an epic in eight volumes which he said were translations from the original Gaelic of Ossian son of Fingal, a legendary warrior

said to have lived in the third century. They were greatly admired for a while by Goethe and Herder, but Dr Johnson and others challenged Macpherson to produce the original MS. Apparently it didn't exist, and Macpherson took refuge in fabrication. A committee was appointed to examine the poems and reported that Macpherson had been guilty of deception. Successive investigations have since confirmed the fraud.

114 Sharp, *English Folk-Song*, chap. I, p. 2.

115 Grimm's *Fairy Tales* were first published in English in 1823 with illustrations by George Cruikshank. Hans Anderson's collection translated into English in 1846 by Mary Howitt, and again in the same year by Caroline Peachey are *not* national folk-tales but his own invention.

116 A great many present-day scholars are of the opinion that the finest specimens of folk-song are to be found in Russia. If this is so, it is what we should expect of such a large peasant population and it is only natural that the U.S.S.R. should foster and subsidize this branch of musical activity. A Russian takes to folk-song as a duck takes to water; and writing for the *Daily Worker*, Karl Frederick Dallas, a former member of the "Young Communist League" and now editor of *Folk-Song*, explained that "it is not surprising that many folk-song clubs have strong links with the 'Young Communist League'. Folk-song is a natural extension of their political belief." Moreover, the debt we owe to Russian initiative was emphasized in a recent letter to a Sunday newspaper in which a correspondent, writing as a Communist said that "when folk-song was in the doldrums in this country, only the Communist party really threw all its weight into its revival!" Cf. Aidan Crawley, *Daily Telegraph*, 14th and 31st December 1963.

117 Dean-Smith, *Malchair's Collection and Dr Crotch's Specimens*, cf. JEFDSS.

118 Sharp, *English Folk-Song*, chap. XII, p. 161.

119 It is a tribute to Davies Gilbert that certain of his specimens, notably Nos. 1, 4, 13, 27, 29, 41, and 72, are included in the latest edition of the *Oxford Book of Carols*. This versatile Cornishman besides being at one time M.P. for Bodmin and an enthusiastic agriculturist, was also a scientist of considerable aptitude, and some of his concepts were embodied in the construction of the new Westminster Bridge and the unique engineering feat

across the Menai Straits. Eastbourne Manor, the scene of so many discoveries of historic value is no longer the family seat; but Miss Davies Gilbert still lives at Birling Manor, an old Gilbert property, and many direct descendants still happily survive in Sussex and Cornwall.

120 Like William Chappell at a later date, both Gilbert and Sandys depended for their material upon the MSS preserved in the libraries and museums of the day, upon pocket-MSS and chap-books, and upon the texts of broadsides – all of which are the well-springs from which the gems of mediaeval piety have come down to us in the twentieth century.

121 Both Gilbert and Sandys took down tunes in Cornwall about the year 1820 from "oral communication" – a sure test that a song is a true folk-song; but Sandys was no musician as is evident from his harmonization of "A Virgin Most Pure" (Ic – Ic – IV – I), and he shows quite clearly that he is incapable of noting down a tune correctly: the carol is wrongly barred in duple time instead of triple measure. Chappell also noted tunes from "oral tradition", but unfortunately a great deal in his *Popular Music of Olden Time* such as "The Miller of the Dee" was spoilt by his attempts to improve them. It is a thousand pities that he did not confine himself to the collecting of English folk-songs at a time when they were to be found in abundance.

It should be remembered that "oral tradition" is not the *only* test of a true folk-song, and as Margaret Dean-Smith says (*Guide*, p. 14): "The difference between the 'folk' and the 'popular' is to be felt rather than explained, and to transmit the distinction to those who do not feel it is well-nigh impossible." You can tell a folk-song as easily as a flower by its scent, and to exclude mediaeval songs from the category of "folk-songs" merely because they have not as yet been noted from "oral communication" is where some folk-song scholars over-reach themselves.

122 This expression derived from the German, seems to have been first used by the Reverend Sabine Baring-Gould instead of "from oral communication". Cf. Dean-Smith, *Guide*, p. 13, footnote.

123 Dean-Smith, "The Preservation of English Folk-Song and Popular Music", Lecture 1949-50 (Extramural Studies, University of London), chap. 5, pp. 38, 39.

124 *Guide*, p. 26, BOE.

125 The finest examples of our ballad literature grew, flourished,

and declined roughly between the years 1350 and 1550 in the border country from the Firth of Forth to the Clyde, and southwards to between Newcastle upon Tyne to St Bee's Head. Although the refrain is not a regular feature of the ballad, the apocryphal element is an infallible sign of Franciscan authorship. Cf. Quiller-Couch, *Studies in Literature*, pp. 24-50.

126 *Guide*, p. 43.

127 Pp. xvi-xvii.

128 The name "Broadwood" is famous among pianoforte manufacturers and in the musical world generally. Every student of the keyboard has been familiar with the sudden change of tone that occurs about D flat below Middle C as the hammers leave the "tre corde" for the "coils". The Broadwood family were the first to attempt to eradicate this blemish.

129 The *Journal* was, and still is the official organ of The English Folk-Dance and Song Society; thirty-five numbers appeared over a period of thirty-two years, and between 1877 and 1909 many of these were edited by Lucy Broadwood herself.

130 Here is the last trace of mediaeval ballet that came to an end with the prohibition of Pope Eugenius IV (1431-1447). By special licence however, the dance was allowed to continue only for as long as the costumes lasted. The astute "maestro de los mocos" has so consistently repaired the garments that the dance is still being performed even today! It can be seen annually at Seville on the feast of Corpus Christi when six boys all under ten years of age, dance before the High Altar to the accompaniment of their castanets. The "maestro" was obliged to lodge the boys in his own house, to feed and clothe them, and to instruct them in the rudiments of music.

131 "It is eight years ago since I began, at first desultorily, to note down and collect English traditional music. During the last half of that period I have spent every available moment of my leisure in country lanes, fields and villages, in the quest of folk-singers and folk-dancers. My collection contains, in round numbers, 1500 tunes. Between twelve and thirteen hundred of these have been captured in Somerset, or, more accurately, in about two thirds of that country which is all I have as yet thoroughly explored. They have been noted down from upwards of 350 singers and instrumentalists." *English Folk-Song*, Introduction, p. xxi.

132 An annotated edition of English folk-songs collected by Sharp in

America was published in two volumes in 1932 under the title *English Folk-Songs from the Southern Appalachians*.

133 "Sharp believed, that there, in the fastnesses of rural England, was the well-spring of English music; tunes of classical beauty which vied with all the most beautiful melody in the world, and traceable to no source other than the minds of unlettered countrymen. He set to work to enable the younger generation to recapture their great heritage of song which their fathers had nearly let slip through their fingers." (Sharp, *English Folk-Song*), "An Appreciation", by Vaughan Williams (1954), pp. vii and viii.

134 We should not overlook the valuable *Carols for Eastertide* published in 1853 by the Rev. J. M. Neale and the Rev. T. Helmore. This was the first recognition since mediaeval times of carols apart from Christmas.

135 It is impossible to overestimate the valuable contribution made by the clergymen of the Church of England towards the revival of the mediaeval carol and the return of carol singing. Had it not been for the scholarship and culture that the devotion of these men had brought to bear from the seclusion of their country retreat, the revival of the carol and of the Christmas message would have been slow indeed.

136 The most recent volume of *Christmas Carols* to have come before the public is that compiled by Elizabeth Poston the well known composer and authority in the field of folk-song (November 1965). In her "Introduction" (page 17) she writes what many of us must have thought but have not had the courage to voice: "The modern 'Festival of Nine Lessons', when it is popularized as, in effect, a concert performance by a crack choir – one that can be made the excuse for the inclusion of poor or indifferent material, however well performed – imposes upon gullible spellbound listeners, who are too ready to accept what they hear, and results in the divorce of carols from the people to whom by rights they belong."

137 The first "Festival of Nine Lessons and Carols" ever to take place in a Roman Catholic Church, was performed with the kind permission of the Parish Priest, the Rev. Gerald Cavanagh, at the church of St Thomas Aquinas, Market Drayton, Salop, in the December of 1956. With the exception of the "Adeste Fideles" the performance consisted entirely of folk-carols sung

unaccompanied by a complement of twelve choristers from Hawkstone Hall under the direction of the author.

138 It is essential for the student to remember that the ultimate product bears little resemblance to the initial composition as launched by the skilled composer.

Index

Only tomes, anthologies, standard works, collections of carols, plays, etc., are within quotes.

† *indicates that a musical illustration is included.*
§ *denotes the first line of a poem or stanza.*
‡ *signifies author's nom de plume.*
* *indicates the title of a poem.*